# THE NINETY YEARS

*A Memoir*

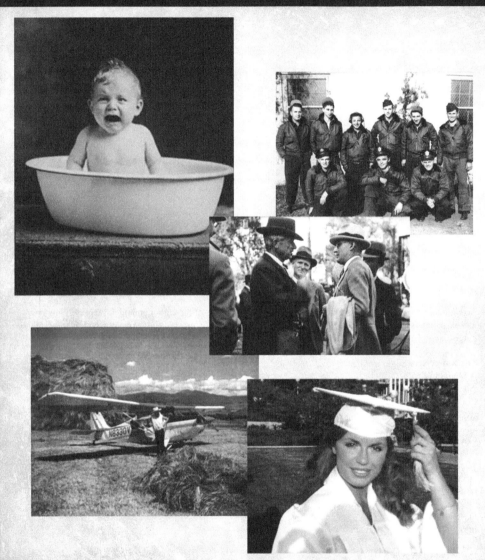

# F. DONALD SOKOL

Outskirts Press, Inc.
http://www.outskirtspress.com

ISBN: 978-1-4787-3301-0

Outskirts Press and the "OP" logo are trademarks belonging to
Outskirts Press, Inc.

PRINTED IN THE UNITED STATES OF AMERICA

# Dedication

*To my beloved wife Debra and our sons
Slade and Taylor, and to my son Douglas
and all the wonderful people who have assisted me to live a wonderful life thus far*

# ACKNOWLEDGEMENTS

My good friend, Tom Gauthier, took the rough and sometimes disjointed manuscript that I had written over the years and transformed it into a cohesive story of what I consider to be an exciting life—to date. Putting down the details of a long and variety filled life is important to me, and Tom has been of vital assistance in its accomplishment.

My beloved wife, Debra, has not been privy to this undertaking by my choice. Of course she'll read the final product and maybe better understand this fellow she threw in with for these great years of our life together. I love you, Debra, and thank you for two great sons, Slade and Taylor.

Also my thanks to Dorro for teaching me how to be a little more civilized in my younger years, and for being the mother of four great children—Evangeline, Douglas, Christine and Mary. Our twenty-three years of marriage produced much joy, and a little misery—c'est la vie.

And to Helen for our five years together—materially productive and one helluva lot of fun and good times. She was 100% all the way.

Special thanks to Julie Johnston, my administrative assistant in my law practice. She not only served me well and true in the practice, but also typed the original draft of this work as I wrote it in bits and pieces. Julie is very patient—and a good friend and assistant to this day.

As you read on you'll know why I want to add special thanks to the instructor pilots of the Army Air Corp in WWII who taught me to fly well enough to survive the war and seventy years of piloting since. Special thanks to Nels Davis, my primary flight instructor, who started me off and got me through solo flight in the beautiful little Ryan PT-22 open cockpit trainer. If it hadn't been for Nels' instruction I wouldn't be alive today.

For another phase of my life, I must acknowledge all of the wonderful law professors at the University of Iowa and Stanford who taught me the legal rules and reasoning that has carried me through a successful legal career—and finally to the bench as Superior Court Judge. Inscribed over the entrance to the iconic and beautiful Santa Barbara Court House in California is, "Reason is the Life of the Law"—a good summation of my law school professors' message.

And last here, but first with me, thank you Jesus for allowing me to see the light and for keeping me safe throughout this often dangerous, but wonderfully fulfilling life. You have allowed me to live.

*Joy of life is doubled when the meaning of your life is acknowledged, shared and enjoyed by others.*

ANON.

*When you put down the good things you ought to have done, and leave out the bad ones you did do well, that's Memoirs.*

WILL ROGERS

# PROLOGUE

The sleek twin engine aircraft flew the length of the picturesque valley then banked east to begin its approach to Susanville Airport in California. As he'd done so many times before the eighty-nine year old pilot smoothly set up for his descent to the runway, wondering for a moment how many landings he'd done since 1943. In fact it had been too many to count for this child of the depression, World War II warrior—pilot, cowboy, attorney, and Judge of the Superior Court. The plane slipped onto the runway, "greased" as pilots say, and taxied to its hangar.

From a broken home in a tiny town, to loving support from an extended family and his own will to push through and win whatever challenge faced him, Frank Donald Sokol set off on a long and serendipitous life's journey. The intervention of a World War provided him with growth, maturity and opportunities that he eagerly embraced. From 35,000 feet in flak filled skies over Germany to knee deep mud on the Oxbow Ranch, from personal triumphs and personal tragedies, Sokol has soared through the heights and rebounded from the lowest of lows.

WW II.

"…Shortly into the bomb run #3 engine shook as flak hit a fuel line. I shut it down and feathered the prop. Then #2 took a hit in an oil line and started streaming oil out behind. About that time the lead ship in our squadron was severely damaged—I was flying on his left wing—and dropped out of formation. This ship had the Squadron Commander in it and as he left the formation he instructed us to salvo the bombs. Then the only ship with a real bombardier (rather than just a toggelier) was hit and dropped out. It was the Group Leader and he ordered the other five ships in our Squadron to salvo also."

"Even after dropping all the bombs we could not maintain level flight. #1 engine had no turbo charger so at that high altitude it was just along for the ride, #2 engine was leaking oil and #3 was feathered, leaving #4 as the sole engine without a problem. With only one good engine out of four we could no longer sustain level flight … we were going down! We really didn't know how far we could get with our damaged ship—go to Russia or Switzerland, or try to make it back to Foggia, our base in Italy. These were the choices. We opted to try to make it home to Foggia, nursing the damaged airplane along in the gradual descent. Then a gunner called out, 'Fighter at three o'clock high!' I looked around and saw my first German fighter, and at that time I had flown 7 missions. Fighter or no fighter, it was apparent that we were not going to make it all the way home. We were losing altitude too quickly …"

This is the story of the full life of a man who tested its extremes and won.

# CONTENTS

**FDS at Eight Months old.    "MAD AS HELL"**

*Chapter 1*

# THE EARLY YEARS

### Maquoketa, Iowa, 1924

This small town, forty miles from the Mississippi River, was typical of small mid-western towns in the 1920's, 30's and 40's. With no factories or industry, the primary business was serving the needs of the farms surrounding the town. The land is very fertile and the primary crop is corn, and most every farm also raised hogs because they do well on corn.

A stucco house at 109 East Judson Street is the beginning of the story for me. When I saw it a few years ago the stucco was quite dirty, things not well attended. A minor detail in the scheme of things in my life which is rapidly, or so it seems, approaching one hundred years.

My very earliest recollection is being in my crib with a nurse looking over the edge of the rail at me, wearing horn rimmed glasses.

I was two years old. My father later told me that I was close to death with a combination of whooping cough and pneumonia.

Back then, our little town of Maquoketa had a by-line: "The Timber City." Today, 2013, their by-line is: "One of a Kind." Progress I guess, but it sure was one of a kind for me growing up.

The town and surrounding area was quite scenic and could be referred to accurately as a typical mid-western farming community. The downtown area had little activity during the week but when Saturday afternoon arrived it was crowded with farmers who traditionally came to town that day of the week. There was always a matinee at the Pastime Theatre on Saturday afternoon, but the primary purpose of the farmers coming to town was to do their weekly shopping.

The surrounding terrain was gently rolling hills with flat lands in between, all covered with corn. The farmers made a good living. Generally speaking, prosperity depended on the size of their farm—the larger the farm, the more prosperous the farmer.

Thinking about it all now, I come to the irrevocable conclusion that a lifetime is nothing more than the memory of a vast multitude of small, insignificant, minor details, a mosaic, the woven fabric of details that make up the cloth, the substance of what we call a "lifetime." When that life mosaic is your own, you want with all your heart to find significance and value in it. Often in hindsight I see some spots, some low points that I perceive as huge mistakes. What a blessing it would be if I could reach back and rectify those mistakes, correct those events, and re-record the saga of my life.

When I began writing this tale—many years ago—I had some personal problems that loomed large, seeming to overwhelm any virtues at the time. It was a shame because I was blessed with high points also, like my two sons and a young beautiful bride, Debra—the epitome of a Georgia Southern Belle. Our mutual love should have eclipsed "problems," as eventually it always does. If I could go back to fix the low spots would that be a good thing? Maybe, but only if I don't have to change or diminish the high spots.

Actually, I believe it to be a pointless exercise because it would not change the present one whit. I report these views to you because at my age they tend to linger just below the surface and need to be properly disposed of.

My name is Frank Donald Sokol, known now to my friends as Don, but with Army Air Corps the ubiquitous rule of "last name, first name, middle initial" I was known as Frank until after WWII.

I've taken on the task of sorting through nine decades of a mishmash of happenstance and serendipity that is my life at the encouragement of friends and family, and a bit of my own curiosity. The task is proving awesome. Early on it seemed to grow as a study in self-centered aggrandizement. Though I can admit to a certain view of my extraordinary self—I quickly will add that I have acted out of what I thought was right at the time.

Come to think of it, in retrospect those actions are the things of which I'm most proud.

Back at 109 East Judson Street events unfolded that shaped my life in many ways. My father, Archibald William Sokol, called Arch or Archie by his friends, was Mayor of Maquoketa for over 10 years. Dad's law office was above the Pastime Theatre and he had a thriving practice for a small town country lawyer. His partner was Frank Kelsey and the firm name was "Kelsey & Sokol." Kelsey was elected trial Judge when I was about in the 4th grade. I'm thinking that my first name probably comes from Frank Kelsey.

Dad was a country lawyer with a high professional rating, but as with most country lawyers he did not accumulate a lot of wealth. He wasn't stingy, just frugal. I recall my father reaching up to the top of a china cabinet in the dining room with money in his hand and leaving it there.

Though out of context, I have a recollection of my dad shaving in the upstairs and only bathroom, his face covered with shaving cream and mad as hell, yelling at my mother.

It seemed that every good thing was tempered by a bad one. Like the day, I was about three, that my father was pulling me in a child's small wagon at a high rate of speed in the front of the "dirty little stucco house." Losing my grip I fell to the ground, landing on my right arm and experiencing a sharp pain as it broke, setting up a trip to Dr. Bowen's office where a real strong yank set the bone the old fashioned way, without even a twitch of his fine mustache. It must have done the job, because the arm healed straight and has never given any trouble.

My father owned some land and one of my fondest memories is going hunting with him on the timber land. Just another of those minor things that came to make more sense as time and events went on, and as already noted, make up the fabric of my life.

During the Depression, about 1931 or 1932 as I recall, the American Savings Bank in Maquoketa failed, as banks were doing in those days. My father had a large investment in it and was on the board of directors, as my grandfather before him. The stock he had was called "double indemnity," because when the bank failed, the directors with stock not only lost their stock but had to match the value of their stock and pay that over to the bank. You can imagine what effect that had on his balance sheet.

My mother, Margaret Maloa Taubman Sokol, kept house for our family of three boys: my older brother Raymond, me and my little brother Richard.

There were others of the extended family that lived nearby. My maternal step-grandfather, Jack Huff, was alive until I was about ten years old. He had been a drummer boy in the Civil War and had one eye shot out. He wore a patch and told me stories of the Civil War and he fancied himself a gambler and played cards all day long. (My paternal great grandfather, whose name was Keller, went away to fight with the Union Army in the Civil War, and never returned, presumed dead in battle. So I have warriors on both sides.)

Just beyond the city limits, my Aunt Eva and Uncle Otto Battles owned one of the most prominent farms in the area. It was called Rosemere, and was well known because Otto Battles showed his Rosemere Angus at all the big fairs and livestock expositions, such as the Chicago International Livestock Exposition and the American Royal at Kansas City. Up until the Second World War he showed more winners at the largest show, Chicago, than any other breeder of Angus cattle. A portrait of Otto V. Battles hangs in the Saddle and Sirloin Club in the Chicago Stockyards, which is quite an honor for a cattleman.

My father and Uncle Otto didn't care much for each other. I think Uncle Otto with only an 8th grade education was a little jealous of my father with his law degree. My father didn't feel Otto was good enough for his sister Eva and at the same time was jealous of all the fame Otto had acquired in the purebred Angus business.

We'll talk more about Uncle Otto later in my story.

Life in our family had long been influenced by the tumultuous relationship of our parents, but the traumatic event that shaped and came to haunt my life to this day hit me like a bombshell from the blue—the fateful day that my mother gathered the three of us, me, my older brother Raymond and baby Richard and set off for Chicago, about 100 miles to the East—the rending of the fabric of my world … our family.

I don't really know what triggered my parent's separation, but it seems to be centered on the birth of Richard, my younger brother. I later learned through many and diverse sources such as talkative playmates and probing relatives, that my mother wanted another baby after me. My father, however, did not. It was shortly after Richard's birth that mother took us to Chicago.

Mother kept us fed working in a dress store called Sally's Frocks and we moved often, living in a succession of apartments. Chicago to a preschooler is a mysterious place and we boys must have been alone much of each day as I can't recall there being a babysitter.

Then one memorable day we moved in with my mother's sister, Aunt Florence, and her husband "Uncle Max" Schmidthoffer. Uncle Max was a physician and he had a fully equipped operating room in the basement of the apartment where he treated or operated on people. The occasional hush-hush late night patients provided me with later speculation that he had some sort of an agreement to stand available to the Chicago mob. Why else have a standby operating room in the basement room of an apartment?

Makes for a good mystery.

At any rate, Uncle Max was a good sort and kind to us children. Sometimes, though, I would overhear the hushed and often heated discussions regarding how long my mother and we three children were going to remain with the Schmidthoffers. I guess it didn't bother me too much because I recall that of the two years we spent in Chicago, the happiest time was with Aunt Florence, Uncle Max, and their two sons, Martin and Arthur.

Their apartment was expensively furnished including a huge grand piano. Raymond, my older brother, used this piano for target practice with a bow and arrow he'd received for Christmas. The arrows had sharp metal tips, and they didn't do much for that mahogany piano. Come to think of it, this target practice is no doubt what hastened our departure from the Schmidthoffer apartment!

My mother and father finally agreed to reconciliation—probably on the telephone.

Speaking of the telephone, I have a vivid recollection of talking to my father and championing my mother's side of their disagreement—me all of four years old. I was pretty mean to him on that call, accusing him of some vague sin against us. What a sad thing that must have been for him to have his little 4 year old son upbraid him on the phone.

Next thing I know back to Maquoketa we traipsed.

Their reconciliation was short-lived.

My mother didn't work in Maquoketa but was entirely dependent on my Dad with no fixed alimony. She did take in "roomers." My mother would have me go to my Dad's office each week and get the money she needed. Such a practice today would be frowned on to say the least, as you well know. He did have an account for us at the grocery store.

I loved and respected my Dad in spite of the family situation.

I was about six years old when we returned and it wasn't long before I was in first grade in the Maquoketa public school. Our house was only one block east of Main Street and across from the Maquoketa High School. The building also housed the Third Ward grade school with grades one through eight.

The school yard was scenic. The brick school building sat on top of the hill and ran a block long. The grounds sloped down to Main

Street and were covered with large trees. I attended grade school there from grades one to three.

It was a happy time for me.

I liked school and Mrs. Hutchins, our first grade teacher, was a kindly woman and a good teacher. But the teacher that is most memorable to me was Mrs. Elsie Hancock. She came to our room to teach penmanship. In those days she traveled around Maquoketa to the town's four grade schools just teaching penmanship. She was a strict disciplinarian, who roamed the aisles with a long wooden ruler in her hand. She would inspect the work of each student and when she saw work she didn't like she rapped the knuckles of the poor performing student—HARD. If anyone talked out of turn, shot a spit ball, made faces or just squirmed too much, she would race down the aisle, grab your ear lobe and YANK HARD.

One did not forget Mrs. Elsie Hancock.

She was all the more memorable because she had taught my Father penmanship some forty years before. I guess that is why she paid special attention to me and favored me a bit. I was scared of her, of course, just like everybody else— really scared of her. I would tell my Dad of this fear, but he would just laugh and tell me she was a sweetheart ... something that I, along with all of my suffering classmates, found very hard to believe.

First grade drifted into second, not hard since they were both in the same room. About this time I fell in love for the first—but not last—time. Her name was Patty Graff. She was an olive-skinned beauty that lived with her folks, the managers of a rest home at the top of Judson Street. Patty didn't pay much attention to me, which I guess made it all the more interesting. It was not until years later, in high school that I confessed to her about my big crush.

Unfortunately, she still wasn't impressed.

**L-R:**

**My maternal Aunt, Mother, Uncle Otto, Grandfather, Father**

# Chapter 2
# MOVING EVENTS

### The Move to Dad's House

The next big event in my life was moving out of mother's house and going to live with my father and grandmother in grandmother's house.

She was a dear lady who made the best plain vanilla cookies in the world, and also made the best toast. Grandma would sit in front of the wood-burning cook stove with the little door open to the fire, holding the toast with an old "Case" fork until it was a golden brown. I must have been fixated on food at that age because I also remember that she was a great noodle-maker, rolling out the dough with plenty of flour on the rolling board, rolling up the flattened dough, and then slicing through the roll to form long strips of noodles. These went into a big iron kettle with some chicken in it, and perhaps some dumplings as well, to become the usual Sunday dinner. I must add that grandma had her own chickens, with the hen house at the back of the garage.

The vegetable garden was in the back yard, tended by my father. He spaded it every spring—until I became old enough to do the spading—and then planted the seeds which produced the most delicious vegetables in the world. At least that my world has ever known. He washed the vegetables under a hydrant that jutted out of the foundation of grandma's house. It had a rock under it to prevent the ground from washing away and the best smells in the world emanated from this washing process. Dad must have been a great gardener because I can still see in my mind's eye all of the great things that came out of it. My favorite was peas.

One of the best things about living at grandma's house was the fact that I got to change grade schools to the Fourth Ward. Housed in a square stone building on the east edge of town, it more closely resembled a country school than the Third Ward where I had started.

There were fewer of us in the classes and the building itself exuded a charm that only very old buildings can do. It was at the Fourth Ward also that I became friends with Jimmy Wendel, soon to be my best buddy.

Jimmy Wendel's dad had a farm on the south edge of town and always had livestock, horses and ponies as well as a few cows and we did a lot of pony riding. Besides Jimmy's farm, we had a lot of room to roam and explore. There were open fields and timber surrounding the area and in those days the farmers did not seem to be concerned about trespassing kids. There weren't that many of us!

Let me tell you more about Jimmy and me. We used to dress alike in knee-height leather lace-up boots and what we would now call "riding britches." They tucked down inside the lace-up boots, a most practical type of footwear for an active boy out in the great outdoors when he wasn't in school. Everywhere either Jimmy or I went, the other went also. He was extra important to me for more reasons. Jimmy's father, Chuck Wendel, was a local used car dealer. As I mentioned earlier, they lived on the outskirts of town on a small farm and dealt in livestock as well as cars—and let Jimmy have ponies to ride.

This was the start of my fascination with cowboys. Jimmy and I would get on his spotted pony, riding "double," and ride it as fast as we could—usually resulting in one or both of us being roughly deposited on the ground.

One evening his dad came home to witness our wild race down a steep hill back to the barn. He couldn't believe what daredevils we had become, but we still got a long lecture about the perils of running down hill on a horse—and also about not riding the pony so hard that its life was imperiled as well as ours.

Boyhood friendships have a way of lasting for life—sometimes. My best buddy friendship with Jimmy only lasted until I married and moved to California to attend law school at Stanford. In hindsight I take the blame. Our closeness seemed to disappear because my thoughts drifted into a vein where I considered myself as "moving up" in the social and economic strata.

I couldn't have been more incorrect, but still even now it comes back to me with overpowering force that rightly or wrongly that is the way my life turned. Now at this juncture I believe one thing I would go back and change is to retain friendships that sadly I cast aside as new chapters of my life unfolded. Even if I believed that there was a good and valid reason why I let a friendship go, I would have been better off to keep more of them.

Now the question arises, if those friendships which I now regret losing would have been kept more closely, would they have diverted my life's course to an extent that I would have arrived at a different point? Would they have changed my life? I'll never know the answer. But I do know that I would not change a thing, not tamper with anything that would alter the present.

## *Moving Back to Mother's House.*

Life in the Fourth Ward only lasted one year as I moved back to my mother's house. I guess I would classify it as being the best year of my grade school life—mostly because of that old school building and its charm. Moving back with my mother sent me back to the Third Ward for Grade Five.

It was at about this time that I developed a fine inferiority complex. My older brother bullied me something fierce. I deeply resented him I guess because he was just older than I and seemed to be the focal point of the family's attention. He just seemed to be always "better" than I. He got things first, and in the logic of a younger brother, was favored, primarily because he was bigger and older and thus a lot smarter.

Oh how I longed for a mother and father that lived together!

I thought that would be paradise itself, if only I had parents that lived together.

## *The Move to Yakima and the Ranch.*

This move I see as the most significant, sending my young life in a new direction. The summer before my eleventh birthday I was invited by my Aunt Eva, my father's sister, to spend a summer with her and Uncle Otto Battles at their home in Yakima, Washington. My brother Raymond had made such a visit three summers before.

As I mentioned earlier Aunt Eva and Uncle Otto were in the

cattle business raising notable registered Angus on their farm on the outskirts of my home town of Maquoketa, Iowa. They also had a partnership ranch a few miles outside the town of Yakima, Washington. This was the ranch where I spent the summer.

Now a whole new world opened up for me, a world that I had only dreamt about while listening to the *Lone Ranger* on the radio. I longed to be a cowboy and now I had my chance to do just that on a real cattle ranch. (This was long before I knew there was such a difference between a purebred operation such as my uncle's and a large commercial cattle ranch (a cow outfit!) such as I myself would in later years own.) My uncle was a large purebred operator in the registered Aberdeen Angus business. (In recent years, the breed name has been changed to just "Angus.") At the time he ran more purebred Angus cattle between the Yakima and Iowa operations than any other breeder in the United States.

At the ranch I was assigned a horse pretty much of my own to ride. It was a mare named Babe and she was the world's best boy's horse. Gentle as she could be, my horse also had lot of life and could run like the wind. She could also catch and turn a cow. Having been used around cattle she pretty much knew what was expected of her before her rider gave her the message. She had the great show-off feature of standing on her hind legs on cue and never going over backwards. Imagine what a thrill for an eleven-year old to have such a horse to parade before his friends on the occasions I would ride her into town where we lived and strut my stuff on that horse.

I liked everything about the cattle business. But best of all, living with my aunt and uncle gave me an almost normal existence as compared to the other kids.

I had both mother and father counterparts.

The fact that they were an uncle and aunt instead of a mother and father seemed secondary to me. My "family," adopted as it was, also was different because *we* had a ranch with all sorts of interesting things to do. This was by way of contrast with my father's profession, a lawyer in a small town such as Maquoketa that meant sitting in a stuffy old office, typing, reading musty law books and sitting in a chair waiting for clients to show up.

Being a cattleman was much more of the manly stuff of which my dreams were made. My days started by riding with my uncle in his 1923 Franklin to the ranch. It was only about five miles from town but it seemed much further back then. When we got to the ranch it was my job to catch our horses and after I got on to it, which didn't take long, to saddle both my uncle's and mine. The ranch foreman, Arnie, or herdsman, Kale, saddled their own. We would then "ride pastures." This meant riding through the various pastures checking on the welfare of the cattle which were a very valuable collection of the best in Angus breeding.

My uncle advertised under the trademark *Rosemere*. He listed it as *The Premier* herd with *unparalleled International* show records. Having shown more winners at Chicago than any other breeder, it was all true at the time.

All of this was pretty heady stuff to me. Uncle Otto had judged most of the big cattle shows around the world. Before he died he had judged the big ones including the show at Perth, Scotland, the homeland of the Angus breed, and the big show at Buenos Aires, the biggest show in South America.

The herdsmen that rode with us were the best in the business and I had my first taste of excellence, professionalism and how much better it is than just being average—or horrors of horrors, second-rate. Cattle became more important than people because with purebred cattle that's just the way it is if you want to get ahead and excel in the business.

My aunt and uncle with no children to occupy their thoughts put the cattle first. At least my Uncle Otto did. I retract the statement as far as my aunt is concerned. She went along with my uncle as far as the cattle were concerned, but basically she was a person-oriented individual.

Of course Uncle Otto was person oriented as well. He could not have achieved all his success without the excellent employees he hired and who stayed with him for many years. He served as president of the American Angus Association and many lesser breed associations He was a columnist with the Angus Journal, with monthly articles for many years. And all of this with only an eighth grade education. He was a "self made man" in every sense of the term. Google "Otto V. Battles and see what appears—several pages even though his death occured in 1967.

When the end of that summer came and I was given the choice to either stay with them or go home to Maquoketa I leapt at the chance to stay with them.

I had never had it so good!

I entered Sixth Grade at the Roosevelt School. It sat at the corner of Summitview and 16th Street, just three blocks from our house at 201 Park Avenue—a classy address at the time. I became known as the "Battles" boy and I could not have been happier. I still got to go to the ranch on Saturdays, and ride my beloved horse, Babe.

When Babe ran she would lay her ears back, hug the ground and run like a grey hound. The practice she had of laying those ears back was unique to her. In my later years I can recall no horse that would lay its ears back flat against the neck and flatten out so far and close to the ground in an attempt to go just as fast as gravity, muscle and wind would allow. She had been a fine polo mount for my Uncle

Otto and in her prime had been one of the best in the West in the game of polo. As far as my Uncle's ex-polo mounts were concerned, she was the only one that had maintained her soundness, including wind, bone and muscle.

She was tough and one of my fondest memories—a first love.

I was especially proud of the fact that she had been a wild horse, rounded up on an Indian Reservation open range destined to serve as dog food as a colt. My uncle bought her for Five Dollars—$1.00 per hundred-weight as she weighed five hundred pounds at purchase. She outperformed almost all, and most certainly out-lasted all of his other expensive horses. She had a *22* brand on her left jaw indicative of having been caught as a colt in 1922. I first rode her in 1935 when I was 11 and she was 13.

We were buddies, just like Jimmy and me.

My first productive work for which I was paid at the ranch was as water boy for the grain threshing crew. I rode Babe and carried water in two canvas water bags hooked on each side of the horn of my saddle. The crew used horse drawn wagons upon which they would hand pitch with pitch-forks the bundles of grain and then haul the loaded wagons in to the big steam threshing machine. Now that was hard work. The bundles probably only weighed twenty-five pounds apiece, but they were on the end of a pitch fork and had to be pitched first on the wagon to a four or five foot height and then off the wagon onto the feeding apron of the thresher. It was hot in the Yakima summer and those perspiring men needed lots of water.

With about twenty-five on the crew it kept me busy riding to carry the water to each one in the field, and then to go fetch more water at a hand operated well pump before they were thirsty again. It was there I learned how important to a field hand it was to have plenty of water available and lots of food, morning, noon, and to a much lesser extent, at night. Suppers at the bunk house where they all slept and ate were mostly composed of left-overs.

I reveled in the atmosphere of life on a real cattle ranch, at least what I conceived to be out of the old West. I was later to learn this was a dude outfit compared to what I would later own myself as it was only five-hundred irrigated acres with perhaps five-hundred cows, and I later would operate on one hundred-fifty thousand plus acres, much of it unfenced, carrying two thousand cows.

There was one outstanding hand on the Yakima ranch that had "cowboyed" on cow outfits and I looked up to him for that reason. Del Board was his name and he knew horses.

My Uncle acquired a filly he named "Madame Butterfly." She was a skittish handful and would buck if given half a chance. Del "green broke" her for my uncle—too green, actually, because my uncle would always ride with an English saddle. Not the best for a skittish horse. One time he started mounting without noting that a stirrup was over the top of the saddle, dropping it to the other side on his way up. That was a big mistake because Butterfly was startled and bucked hard enough so he was off immediately and fell hard on the back of his head. He had to crawl in to Headquarters for assistance, was taken to the hospital and barely survived the concussion. They had to cut his boots off, something I would have done to myself in later years more than once as I got into big time cattle ranching and real buckarooing.

Uncle Otto was actually a minority partner in the Yakima ranching operation which operated under the name and style of *Congdon & Battles*. Congdon was the name of a Duluth mining family who had gone into partnership with my uncle in the purebred Angus business shortly before 1920.

The original Congdon, Chester, the founder of the fortune, died in the early years of the partnership, leaving my uncle dealing with sons and the family trust. This was not a very satisfactory arrangement because the Trust was always dissatisfied with the losses accumulated by the cattle business. Eventually they felt they had lost enough money and notified Uncle Otto in 1938 to sell the cattle as they were withdrawing from the business. This about broke his heart, because he had put so much of his life into the business. He arranged to have all the cattle shipped to Iowa where there was a better market and staged the Angus sale of the century up to that date in 1938. After that dispersion sale he never again operated on the scale that he had with the Congdons, but he actually made more money due to increasing value of the farm lands upon which he ran his cattle.

**Foreground: Left, Will Rogers, Uncle Otto Battles**

**Photo taken on set of the movie "State Fair in Des Moines, Iowa.**

## Chapter 3

# RETURN TO IOWA

### *High School Days and Beyond*

It was in the fall of 1940 that Uncle Otto gave me the choice of returning to Maquoketa to my parents, by that time divorced, or remaining with them in Yakima. I chose to go to Maquoketa, a decision which I later regretted fervently when I realized how really crummy that life was in a small town in Iowa compared to life on a cattle ranch in the west—and more importantly with an aunt and uncle who lived together and served as my own mother and father.

I would cry myself to sleep at night in the small house on Judson Street where my mother still lived with my two brothers and it didn't take me long to move out of that house and move in with my father and grandmother again where the house was neater and cleaner by far. This was something I had gotten used to with my aunt's immaculate housekeeping and much more of a structured and "higher-class" existence. I had always favored my father and after my Yakima experience it became more pronounced. My mother never really forgave me for moving out on her. From that day on I stayed with my father even after grandmother died and he and I lived alone. That is the way high school at Maquoketa went as far as living arrangements were concerned.

Jimmy was still my buddy in High School and we had some great times together. We both played clarinets in the marching and concert bands. The typing team to which we both belonged was especially fun because as clarinet players we seemed to have a digital dexterity on typewriters that was outstanding. Also, we were the only boys on the typing team which we really enjoyed after getting deeply into matters sexual. We liked girls. That was why we tried out for and made the typing team—primarily so we could travel around Iowa with the girls attending typing contests and doing pretty well—both with the typing and with the girls.

In the summer I would work for my uncle on the Iowa farm which he continued to own and operate. Back with my beloved black cattle which I had truly grown attached to. I loved to saddle up and ride those pastures, inspecting the cattle and doing anything that was necessary to take care of them.

He had shipped Madame Butterfly, the great but skittish horse, back to Iowa from Yakima. I loved to ride her and her brother, Firefly, showing off to my friends what a cowboy I was—which I wasn't yet, but it was fun pretending.

Because of my experience in the west I considered myself a lot different and a lot better than the average Iowa school boy. Except for Jimmy, my buddy, I didn't have a large group of friends. But we had fun together. We did all the absolutely insane things boys do.

Especially with the girls—I won't go into details as they could be painful for the living.

Perhaps another day.

Because I started this story with the idea to be absolutely truthful, now I ask is this possible? Yes, but only at the expense of civility! I don't know that I'm ready for that just yet. I will say that my first sexual experience was on a double date with Jimmy. We had somehow managed to get two gals in my father's 1940 Chrysler Royal, a pretty neat machine. It was night, of course, and we parked on a high hill on a back road. The trip there was for the express purpose of losing my virginity. Jimmy, much to my chagrin, had lost his first with an English teacher who had taken him and another schoolmate on during an extemporaneous outing!

I withdrew with my companion from the front seat of the Chrysler to the rear of the car—outside—where I unceremoniously and, I fear roughly, threw her to the ground. Not that she wasn't willing—nay I believe she was committed to the plan before we had left town. I had intelligently found a condom someplace and we did it right there on the ground. But I worried for months afterward that something had gone wrong and that the gal was pregnant. It was a classic case of the girl looking terrible the day afterwards and it was all over school the next day what had transpired on that hill. I was teased for months afterwards, but it taught me a lesson that I tended to forget in later years—especially under the influence of alcohol. As Jim's dad put it, "Never go to bed with a gal that you would not want to face across the breakfast table the next morning."

Excellent advice.

I guess those high school football games, in which I played right end, and Jimmy played guard, will have to stand out as a high point for high school experiences. My "steady" girlfriend was the lead drum majorette and how we made love! It really wasn't that great—in her folk's living room after they had gone to bed or in the back or front seat of my dad's car—but it sufficed at the time. In spades. I was constantly bragging to my buddy Jimmy about all the sex I was getting. So much so that I also suggested that he date her younger sister who was fourteen at the time.

He did, and then married her when she was fifteen, and remained married to the day he died at age seventy-five!

To demonstrate the trouble teenage boys can get into, I must mention one spring vacation canoe trip Jim and I took. We decided the boat we needed for this trip to the headwaters of the Maquoketa River was the local trial court Judge's "Old Town" canoe. The fact that it was in a locked boat house, that we didn't know the Judge, and we had no intention of asking his permission to use the boat did not seem important. We sneaked into his boat house and took that canoe in the dead of night, paddled it for six days to the headwaters of the Maquoketa River and back, returned the boat, and no one was the wiser until years later when I confessed to my dad.

I don't know whether Jim ever told anyone.

One weekend in our high school senior year, Jim and I went camping at my dad's timber land, sleeping in an abandoned wood-cutter's cabin. When we got home Sunday afternoon, I can remember my dad coming out on the back porch and calling out to us that Pearl Harbor had been attacked and the country was at war.

A few months later both of us matriculated at the University of Iowa—I for a summer session in 1942, and Jimmy in the fall. I had pledged my dad's fraternity, Beta Theta Pi, one of the highlights of my young life. When my dad had driven me to Iowa City to install me at the Beta house, I was impressed because the boys at the house were mostly from the larger Iowa cities. I was generally considered a "country bumpkin" or "hick."

So as with any pledge from a small town, the "actives" took it upon themselves to teach us the facts of University life and what was expected of us. This was a growth experience for me, although painful. And I do mean physically painful because the "actives" chose to enforce their beliefs through the use of large wooden paddles applied to our behinds with considerable force. They would line us up in the Great Hall and individually berate us for minor or imagined infractions of the House rules, whatever they might be. How serious the infraction determined how many swats we received from the paddle.

It not only hurt physically, but they were psychological blows as well. The verbal abuse heaped upon us bordered on the sadistic.

Our pledge master, as he was called, later went on to a distinguished law career, the Federal bench and counsel to the U.S. Senate for special prosecutions. I had imagined that he was so mean that he would not survive long with the temper that he displayed to us as pledges. This shows how wrong one can be in such matters.

College was a tremendous experience, especially in those first few months in the Beta house. The girls in College were more sophisticated, and smarter, but in later years I was to question the advisability of getting involved with intellectual ladies. The simpler, uneducated, but with native intelligence seemed to be much preferable. The ideal is to find the right one in the beginning, from the same social strata, of similar interests, including both intellectual and physical, and stay with her for life.

Those that are fortunate enough to get the job done in the first attempt are lucky indeed.

My dad was so proud that I was in the Beta house and we

corresponded regularly. He was an excellent piano player and played all the fraternity songs. He wore his Beta Theta Pi ring with the solitary diamond in the middle until the day he died and was buried with it still on his finger.

With my mother, the contacts were few and far between for which I regret. The years with my aunt and uncle had completely centered my attention on my Dad's side of the family.

## Chapter 4

# DECEMBER 7, 1941—THE WAR

On that cold winter day on our return from the camping trip that Jimmy and I were told about Pearl Harbor, my initial reaction was to want to enlist.

I was 17 years old.

### *My Enlistment*

In January 1943 at age 18 I did enlist in the Army Air Corps because I considered it to be the most glamorous branch of the service. Those songs about the silver wings got to me.

I went to Des Moines for the entrance examinations during the period reserved for the regular initiation into the Beta fraternity, but I had not realized this until I returned. I was heart-broken, because I knew how much it meant to my father and to me to be an "active" Beta. I literally cried about it to the President of the fraternity. As a result of my tears they held a special initiation just for me, which I appreciate to this day. Our old saying, "Once a Beta, always a Beta," is a true one. The feeling of fraternity brothers for each other can be very real and wholesome, which it was in my case.

In February of 1943, after completion of my first semester's college work, I went home to Maquoketa briefly before packing to report to the Army. On the day I was set to leave, Jimmy and I drank a lot of beer. We didn't want to stop! Dad called us at the beer joint to remind me we needed to get started for the train station, about fifteen miles away. I finally showed up at Dad's house and insisted on doing the driving.

The train station was located in the village of Delmar and I drove as fast as the Chrysler would go, seeing how close I could come to the bridge abutments and doing about 90 mph. We made it safely and Dad put me on the train for my reporting point—Shepherd Field, Wichita Falls, Texas.

A great change was about to come into my life. When I arrived at the base, they put me in a barracks filled with mostly Indians from Oklahoma. Choctaws, as I recall. The barracks were across from the P.X. (Post Exchange) where the 3.2 beer was sold, very weak stuff. It was strong enough, though, to get those Indians intoxicated most every night and they would troop through that barracks, waking us to the wild yells of drunken Indians.

Basic training was mostly a matter of lots of calisthenics. I became sunburned from having to do the calisthenics without a shirt in the hot Texas sun. The skin literally peeled from my back. It is a wonder I survived, but better days were in store for me.

We were shipped one bright lucky day to Tempe, Arizona, where the Air Corps had a College Training Detachment (CTD). Basically, we went to college for a few months, about three, did lots more calisthenics, and were introduced to flying in airplanes known as

*Interstate Cadets.* This was my first aerial experience and on the first flight I got airsick. I managed to get through the course okay, although it did not even include a solo flight.

That was to come later in the regular Primary Flight Training in California.

After Tempe we were shipped to Santa Ana, California, for pre-flight training, which included a lot of math and navigation. We were not allowed off the base for the first thirty days and it seemed like a veritable prison. Discipline was extra tough and the hazing was somewhat of a replay of what we got at the Beta house as pledges—but without the paddles. The base at Santa Ana was huge, and one soon faced the reality that each one of us was such a small grain of sand in the total war effort.

Our heroes were the guys flying P-38's out of Orange County Air Base next door to Santa Ana. They would "rat-race" and do their acrobatic routine all day long while we were marching, drilling, doing calisthenics and standing at attention.

The one big event in my life during pre-flight training was the weekend that a friend of my Aunt Eva and Uncle Otto Battles, a man named G. Harold Janeway, a Los Angeles attorney, treated me to a visit to his ranch near Palomar, California. We slept in sleeping bags outside beside his swimming pool and rode horseback. It was a fantastic visit for me. Especially with the horseback riding. I was still dreaming of an old fashioned cow outfit—like the Oxbow Ranch. I'd heard of the Oxbow when one of the owners, Sherm Guttridge, visited my Uncle in Yakima, buying range bulls for the Prairie City, Oregon outfit.

(Unknown to me then, in later years I was to own and operate my dream—The Oxbow.)

## *Primary Flight Training with Real Aircraft*

From Santa Ana we really got lucky and were shipped to King City, California. Our base was the Mesa Del Ray Air Field, a civilian operated primary flight training operation. It was like a country club compared to anything the Army Air Corps had to offer.

We were introduced to a real airplane, the Ryan PT-22, powered by a 185 horse power five cylinder Kinner engine. My first flight ended in disaster, because the instructor did some unexpected (to me) acrobatics, causing my uneducated stomach to disgorge its contents. However, I was able to mask most of my sickness by swallowing vomit, a trick I used a couple of more times before I became completely used to flight. Air sickness was a hurtle that a lot of us had to overcome, and which I was able to do successfully, without too much trouble.

Oh! The wonderful world of flight.

With some it is just another experience.

With me it became a passion. Something I really loved to do.

There was an element of fear, of course, but nothing that a little time tended to ease.

Later, in mortal combat in the skies of Europe, I was to discover what real fear is.

As we gradually achieved flight status at Mesa Del Rey we commenced a personal growth that was to last a lifetime, and is still with me: that of growth into a better pilot. The fact of the matter is that growth never stops as long as one flies an airplane as a pilot. Every flight is a new challenge, big or small, and every one is a little different, presenting a different challenge.

At King City I learned to drink pretty well at the King Bean Tavern. If there was a kind of rotgut that I didn't try, I don't know what it was. I particularly remember the discovery of the taste of

Scotch and those terrible times when one gets sick after imbibing too much.

I felt at home in King City because it had a definite cowboy atmosphere to it and that was a big part of my life. Also, Aunt Eva and Uncle Otto had purchased a ranch in the Santa Ynez Valley, close by Los Olivos, California, about one hundred-fifty miles South, and they came up to visit me. I felt like the big war hero already, flying those PT-22's, and the sky was full of them, which entertained my aunt and uncle. Otto was impressed with my having become an aviation cadet and that I was well on my way to becoming a full-fledged pilot.

Adding greatly to the "at home" feeling, in 1943 Aunt Eva and Uncle Otto invited me and a cadet friend, Dick Smith, down to their ranch for Christmas. They were staying at Mattei's Tavern in Los Olivos, California, a great old Inn that had been in the Mattei family since stagecoach days.

I can still remember putting the ornament on the top of the Christmas tree, an angel—and Aunt Eva commenting on my lifting the angel's skirt as I was putting her on the top of the tree.

## The Real World of Flight

We were standing retreat one evening by the flagpole at Mesa Del Rey base when a P-38 flew overhead trailing smoke from one engine. It made a left turn to land at one end of the field but did not touch down until the last third of the runway, toward the west where the edge of the mesa ended. (A mesa is a flat-topped hill that drops steeply on all sides and the field got its name, *Mesa of the King*, from this topographical feature.)

We all broke formation and ran the 1/4 mile to the field, reaching there just as the "38" went off the edge of the mesa.

There was a resounding explosion.

I'll never forget the ground shaking beneath my feet.

I felt terrible, for surely the pilot had been killed.

We stood at the formation ground by the airfield, stunned and shaking our heads for a few minutes as the wail of the siren on the ambulance racing toward the crash site faded.

In about five minutes the ambulance came back to where we stood and the rear door opened. Out jumped a leather-jacketed Second lieutenant—the pilot of the '38.

We were astonished and impressed with the survivability of an airplane crash.

I remember it as a big boost to morale.

I recall no fatalities while I was in Primary Flight Training, but there had been quite a few prior to our arrival and there would be more after we left. Training pilots in a hurry as they did in those days, en masse, could only be classified as risky business. Each class would take off together at the same time, perhaps fifty to seventy-five airplanes, all piloted by green cadets—student pilots. Believe me, it was necessary to have your eyes open in order to stay alive.

After about ten hours of dual instruction my instructor, Nels Davis, turned me loose for my first solo, with the standard words, "I'm getting out of this thing before you kill us both."

Nels was a big, heavy-set fellow with a pilot's hairline mustache—very dashing, and he always smoked a cigarette immediately after getting out of the airplane.

It sure looked empty and blank up in that front cockpit without him there. I still remember how light the airplane felt on take-off without him in the front seat.

Bouncing it in for an acceptable first landing, I soared back into the sky and came around for two more landings as was the custom.

The next day we were headed back to that same auxiliary field for more solo flight when we had a memorable experience. Nels and I entered the traffic pattern in a left turn which he was executing, then turned for a right down wind pattern parallel to the runway. While Nels was flying he was "chewing me out" for something I had done wrong.

Suddenly something caught my attention.

Out of the right corner of my eye I spotted another PT-22 above and sliding toward us—perhaps 50 feet away.

Nels had his head down, concentrating on chewing me out.

I knew not what to do! With more experience I would have just "dumped the stick" (full forward) which was right between my legs. But at that time when my instructor was flying the plane I didn't fool with the controls—especially since he was in the process of chewing me out. I didn't yet have enough maturity to know what to do, but the desire to survive took over to the extent that, in a millisecond I reached up and hit his shoulder with my right hand and at the same time gestured wildly toward the airplane almost on top of us.

Nels dumped the stick and the other plane slid overhead so close that I could read the instruments inside its cockpit, the tail wheel just missing our heads. Nels didn't seem to react, but he landed the airplane, got out, lit his usual cigarette, looked in my eyes and said, "I guess you wouldn't know how close that was, but that time it took two of us. Do you feel like soloing again today?"

Of course, my response was, "sure!" and off I went.

Nels signaled me in after one landing instead of the usual three and we went straight back to the home field. He was still shaken there too. With my inexperience I didn't realize how close we had come to death.

I didn't know it at the time, but I was to come lots closer to it later on in the flak-filled skies of Germany.

## *On to Basic Flight Training*

Finally, after about three months, we completed the Primary Flight Training Course. It was with a degree of sadness that I left King City. It had been a good place. The cadets in my class were sent to many different fields for the next step in our training.

I was sent to Lemoore Army Air Base near Lemoore, California. For some reason I will never forget the trip over the hills from King City to Lemoore. It was a relatively short bus ride of perhaps one hundred miles, but maybe it is memorable because it went through cattle country on the way—the Kettlemen Hills.

At Lemoore Army Air Base we were obviously back in the real Army again. Gone was the country club atmosphere of the civilian-contracted flying school at King City—where we actually had girls serving the food in the mess hall. At Lemoore, we once again were eating in a regular old Army mess hall.

What we really looked forward to at Lemoore was the chance to fly a bigger and better airplane—the Consolidated Vultee BT-15. We definitely moved up in the world from the PT-22 with this plane—it was *not* open cockpit.

At King City we had civilian instructors with Army check pilots. At Lemoore all of the instructors were Army pilots, who were much less sympathetic with the problems of cadets. I should mention in this regard that Nels, my instructor at King City, had really taken an interest in me after the incident in which we almost had the mid-air collision. He definitely indicated that I had saved both of our lives that time. He had about five cadets to instruct and I was his favorite after the near-miss. He indicated that in his opinion I was a good pilot, which pleased me greatly. When one civilian check pilot on my first check ride had given me a failing grade, Nels couldn't understand it. As was the custom, I was given another ride by an Army check pilot and passed with "flying colors." When the ride was finished I remember the Army instructor looked me straight in the eye and said, "That was a good ride, Mister." That made my day because if I had flunked that Army re-check ride it would have ended my Army flying career. The worst thing, of course, that could happen to a cadet was to be "washed out." Horror of horrors, but it happened to about 40% of the class.

That Vultee BT-15 aircraft was a clunker in a way as it didn't have enough power for that big fuselage. As I recall it had a 450 hp Wright engine and was originally designed as a dive bomber with a lot more power. Its most distinguishing characteristic was its reluctance to recover from a spin. It just wouldn't stop spinning after the normal recovery was executed with the controls, usually making another turn or so.

I can't blame the instructors who, understandably, didn't like to demonstrate spins. The usual procedure was to show a cadet one spin and let it go at that. I mustered enough courage to do one once in a while on solo flights. It was a breath-taking maneuver at best.

Deadly stupid at worst.

We had been introduced to a few acrobatic maneuvers such as snap-rolls and spins in Primary Training. We now added more in Basic, but it was not emphasized at all. This was probably a good thing for me because I still had a tendency toward air-sickness when doing acrobatics. I've never gotten completely over this tendency, even after over twelve thousand hours of flight that I've logged since.

One of the outstanding things about any Basic training field in those days was the noise of those engines. It had to be the noisiest single-engine airplane ever built. On takeoff its two-speed prop governor was set by the pilot to low-pitch (high RPM) for the climb and then pulled back into high-pitch for cruise. All the work close to the ground was done in high pitch so it made for a noisy place at the home base with several hundred airplanes in the air at the same time.

One of the most dangerous phases of training was the beginning of night-flight. There were fatalities in most every class when night flying started. We were taught "black-out" landings with no lights whatsoever. This was an especially hazardous part of the training. We were also introduced to formation flying, to which I took an immediate liking. This was to come in handy later in combat where close formation was essential to the success of the mission to concentrate both the fire power of the airplanes against enemy attack and the bomb pattern on the target: The closer the formation, the closer the pattern of bombs for complete destruction of the target.

Our alcohol drinking in Basic was done mainly in Hanford, a few miles distant. It was just standard operating procedure (SOP) to go into town whenever we were allowed a pass and drink to excess—polite for get drunk. Back then I smoked as did most of the cadets and always more so when drinking. But when one is young, the hangover isn't so bad – at least in retrospect.

Throughout cadet training I got along fine with my instructors with one exception. That was in Basic training. I don't recall all the circumstances, but essentially the incident occurred one day as I reported for a flying session along with some other cadets to our instructor, whose name I don't remember. I don't believe I had ever had any difficulty with this particular instructor, but that day he must have gotten up on the wrong side of the bed. As I walked up to him, he took one look at me and started to chew me out because there were some food stains on the left-front of my flying suit, near the zipper. I didn't know they were there, but I really felt foolish standing there at attention while he ranted away at my lack of military neatness and polish with respect to dress. Looking back on this small incident, which was never repeated, I believe it is why, when I graduated from flight training I was made a "flight officer" rather than second lieutenant.

This "disgrace"—being made a "flight officer" and given blue and gold insignia bars rather than the second lieutenant's straight gold bars—was reserved for those cadets who were deficient in some respect, usually because of lack of military bearing or maturity.

The only incident or event I have ever been able to remember when I had any difficulty in the discipline department was this one—a small item in basic when I wore a soiled flight suit! I guess I learned that it takes very little sometimes to make a big difference. I considered the difference in being graduated as a flight officer rather than a second lieutenant to be one of the big disappointments of my life.

Of course, a few months later I was made a second lieutenant, and then first lieutenant overseas before the war ended. So it certainly wasn't that much of an earth-shattering event by any means, but it did seem important at the time.

We took up instrument flying in basic training, which was a big thing. In those days the "hood" under which one flew to simulate instrument flight was a piece of black cloth in the back of the BT-15 which pulled up over the head of the cadet so he couldn't see out. It was much more effective than the little eye shade-type hoods that are in use now for simulated flight. The old type of hood made it impossible to see anything, so flying became a matter of having to rely solely on the instruments.

That was the whole point.

### *Advanced Flight Training*

Completing Basic Flight Training in early 1944 we left Lemoore, California for Marfa, Texas, and advanced twin engine training. By now I had decided that multi-engine airplanes were the ones I wanted to fly. Perhaps this was because I did not exactly cotton to aerobatics, which were emphasized in the single-engine advanced fighter schools. Subject to motion sickness when the plane was upside down or gyrating through the sky in unusual attitudes, I was just thankful that I could handle all of the mildly acrobatic maneuvers, such as spins and stalls, without getting too sick.

Truly believing that if I could only achieve status as a full-fledged Air Corps pilot, and that would literally put me on top of the world, I requested and was granted my twin-engine advanced training preference.

Marfa, Texas, was and is a small livestock town in West Texas. The sort of cowboy town atmosphere I'd always enjoyed. The base, however, was an architectural disaster—low, one-story tar paper shacks heated by coal-burning pot-bellied stoves. With one at each end of the barracks, the coal-burning led to an atmosphere polluted by coal smoke and dirt.

As cadets in twin-engine advanced training we led an exciting life. Looking forward to graduation in May gave us a near-term goal for which to work toward. The airplanes we flew were AT-17's also known as "Cessna Bobcats."

They also suffered the indignities of other names such as "Bamboo Bombers."

The Bamboo Bomber actually has a spruce wood frame. And it

wasn't a bomber, but a transport plane used to shuttle the military's top brass and of course to train us pilots who would go on to fly actual bombers during the war. There was no way one of them would fly on one engine, even with their 220 horsepower Jacobs—also known as "Shaky Jakes."

The first thing they taught us was how to get out in a hurry if one caught on fire. Made of wood and fabric, think World War I, they really burned quickly when they caught on fire—which was not all that uncommon. We were taught how to bail out the rear and only door in a just a few quick movements. It's memories like this that seem to stick with us—the life and death kind of which I have experienced quite a few.

As a matter of fact, looking back at my life, the really close brushes with death are what stand out along with the really good things which have happened—such as making love.

I guess the good things stand out for obvious reasons and the brushes with death stand out because they threaten to take away or obliterate the good times.

There is something about danger and calculated risk that has always fascinated me. I must confess that I have been drawn to it—at least the calculated risk. I find it in flying, cowboying, trying law suits in court and skiing. I believe the reason is that such moments of danger require complete concentration and focus to the exclusion of all other cares, thereby obliterating all other problems for that particular moment in time. Taking on something demanding and dangerous and performing well and skillfully is the best.

After one got on to the flight characteristics of the bamboo bomber the flying in Advanced School was not difficult. Being very light, made out of wood and fabric, our aircraft tended to float on landing if you didn't keep the air speed under control. I had no trouble flying the bird and was the favorite cadet in our class with the instructor—a brag point looking back.

The night formation flights really stand out in my memory.

The trick on a dark night was to move in as closely as possible so that the navigation light on your wing tip would light up the other airplane. This required a delicate touch. The instructors were understandably nervous about night formation flight because it was impossible for them to forget that those planes so close on the right and left were being flown by novice formation pilots. The accident rate during these times was understandably quite high. The standing joke was that the instructor would tell his class of cadets to rendezvous over Cathedral Mountain, a prominent landmark at 10 PM.

But if it was a dark night the instructor in his airplane would never show up and there would just be a bunch of cadets out there circling around Cathedral Mountain waiting and watching—until the class time was up and back to the base they would go.

The night cross-country flights were fun. We flew the "light lines," just like air mail pilots of old. These beacons were placed along the airways in a line with each flashing a Morse code identifying its geographic position.

On a clear night they were pretty to watch.

**USAAC Private FDS in Basic Training**

**Aviation Cadet FDS,**
**Primary Flight Training, Ryan PT-22**

# *Chapter 5*

# MY SILVER WINGS

### *Graduation Day Arrives*

May 15, 1943, a day that I can't recall any more deserving of celebration than that one.

I don't remember exactly how I celebrated, but I'm sure it entailed lots of drinking because that we how we always celebrated in those days. Maybe a certain amount of alcohol is useful for such purposes and I was certainly convinced of it at that time.

My big disappointment, as I've already indicated, was graduating as a flight officer, rather than as a second lieutenant. The title "F/O" was also synonymous with "f_ _ _ - off," referring to the fact that something was lacking or you would have graduated a second lieutenant—big embarrassment.

But it was an embarrassment that few of the folks at home understood.

Rank was not even noticed if one had those "silver wings" on one's dress tunic.

I do remember how proud I was to return to Maquoketa wearing the officer's garb and sporting those beautiful wings. Nothing in my life then gave me more satisfaction. Of course, it was all an ego trip—but a little more practical since the gals really went for the guys wearing the silver wings. Another mark of a pilot was the "fifty mission crush" on the officer's hat. The style was created by removing the cardboard stiffener from the top of the hat and letting it droop down toward the ears—a sort of "go-to-hell" look that was strictly "cool" in today's terminology. Actually, this hat treatment also had a practical side. When worn in the cockpit with earphones over the top of the hat the grommet would interfere.

The more hours one had in this mode the more the crush in the hat!

So the hats of the real veteran pilots really had a droop—ergo, the fifty mission crush.

### The Hot Pilot

I had a really good time showing off the flight officer's bars, uniform and silver wings to the family and girls.

But the glory was short-lived—maybe a week.

At graduation time I had been assigned, much to my chagrin, to co-pilot training on B-17 bombers and had orders to report to Kingman, Arizona. My preference was for B-25 pilot training, but B-17 co-pilots were needed more than B-25 pilots. So in addition to the flight officer commission rather than second lieutenant, there was the further disappointment in being assigned to co-pilot training.

Frankly, however, the joy and pride of being made an officer, even a flight officer, and getting those beautiful silver wings more than made up for other disappointments.

## *Flying the Bomber*

The first take-off in a B-17 was a real thrill. It seemed the most massive thing in the sky. At the time only the B-29 was bigger. We flew gunners on practice flights while we were learning the airplane. We sometimes used camera guns and "fired" on AT-6's flying pursuit curves on us. Other times the gunners fired real live ammunition at sleeve targets towed by the AT-6's. It was sort of boring work. It got so boring, in fact, that when they told us that we were going to a place called Yucca where there was an auxiliary strip to camp out for a week or two in the desert, a friend of mine and I decided to have our tonsils removed instead of going to Yucca.

Now, the tonsils really did need removing, but that thought of having to stay at Yucca provided the impetus for us to have the operation.

The tonsil operation is a vivid memory because they lined us up in a hallway in wheel chairs—like an assembly-line. As I recall there were at least five or six of us in the hallway and the surgeon took a very few minutes on each of us, using a local anesthetic only.

For years afterwards any doctor who looked in my throat exclaimed something like, "My God, who did this?"

We were at Kingman for about three months and then shipped to McDill Field, Tampa, Florida—from the desert to the tropics.

It was still summer in Florida and it rained several times every day while the temperature was running in the 100's. Everything steamed. Just walk one block and your uniform was soaked through with perspiration. One of the memories of Tampa that stands out is the pompano fish, cooked in paper at the Columbia Restaurant in

Ybor City, an old section of the city of Tampa.

At McDill, we got lots of training in formation flying, something I always enjoyed, and we did lots of night flying.

One night especially always stands out in my memory.

We were to fly to Miami from Tampa and on the way there was a very dark cloud directly in our path of flight. Actually it was a very black cumulonimbus cloud—a thunderhead capable of heavy rains and raging winds. We were too inexperienced to know any better than to fly right into the thing.

Zowie!

What things we discovered in that cloud.

It had so much rain inside that it was like turning the ship into a submarine. Controllability of the plane, even with two of us using all our strength on the controls, was a big problem. We were at the mercy of the tremendous forces in that cloud. Just when we were almost sure that we were doomed, we broke out into brilliant clear moonlight in smooth air and right over Miami—something that brought to my mind at the time the song *Moon Over Miami*, and still does when I recall this experience.

Another day we were flying formation with our aircraft "in the slot"—nose of my plane tucked right under the tail of another. We were flying directly into the sun when suddenly I lost my vision completely. The other pilot had to take over the controls. It took me several hours to recover and I have always felt that any subsequent eye trouble I had were related to this experience.

At McDill Field we were assigned to combat crews—three commissioned officers (the pilot or airplane commander, co-pilot and navigator) and six non-commissioned enlisted men (toggelier substituting for bombardier, radio man, two waist gunners, ball turret gunner and tail gunner).

Let me say at the outset with respect to a bomber combat crew, the relationship between the pilot and co-pilot is very important—especially when you are the co-pilot as I was.

The pilot with whom I was assigned was Archibald Freebairn, a tall, blue eyed, but dark haired young man. It was apparent to me after flying with him a few times that he was an extremely poor pilot. He just couldn't seem to get anything right. He did manage to get the airplane around the patch and to fly loose, sloppy formations in a rough, jerky fashion. But there was absolutely no finesse to him as a pilot. Actually, he was not such a bad fellow and I probably didn't like him for one reason only—that was because he was the airplane commander instead of me. But I still feel there is an element of truth in what I just related concerning his piloting.

I will say that he did get better as a pilot after he had flown with me for a while in combat. He learned to fly formation. But in the "clutch" situations in which we found ourselves later on he really did muff it badly. If he is still alive and reads this, all I can say is "Sorry, Archie."

But I am telling it like I saw it to the best of my ability.

**2<sup>nd</sup> Lieutenant Sokol, USAAC 1944**

**B-17 Air Crew on flight to Europe:**

Kneeling, Frank Sokol, Archibald Freebairn, Paul Havlick;

Standing, William Coleman, John Schultheres, Albert Brodsko, Raymond

Huckstaedt, Myron Brown and Arthur Harmon

# Chapter 6

# THE FLIGHT OVERSEAS TO COMBAT

We completed our operational training at MacDill Field in about two months and were ready to be assigned to combat posts in specific Groups and Squadrons overseas. The first stop was Savannah, Georgia to pick up our brand-new B-17 with a full complement of combat armament. She really looked beautiful to us after the war-weary airplanes we had been flying in training. We were issued all sorts of interesting gear, like 45 caliber automatics in shoulder holsters, new flight clothes, and even a brand-new chronometer watch. Needless to say, it was all very thrilling.

At last our training had come to fruition and we were going to a combat theatre of operation. What a thrill for a country boy from Iowa. Little did we realize fully that we were headed for an area in which our lives had become the property of Uncle Sam and when he said "go there to bomb," we had to go—even though it meant death would become a very distinct possibility and often was a reality. But at the time we got all those new duds and equipment, the glamour side of the situation was foremost in our minds.

There was one item of equipment that I didn't fully understand—an inhaler. I had a cold at the time and thought it was for clearing the nasal passages. Actually, it was a Benzedrine inhaler to be used for staying awake when we were forced to go without sleep. As I kept treating that cold with the Benzedrine inhaler I couldn't understand why I was unable to sleep for several nights. I finally tumbled on to what the problem was.

Within a few days we were in the sky in our brand new B-17 and opening a large manila envelope which contained our secret orders regarding what our destination was to be. When we took off, we knew that the first landing was to be at Goose Bay, Labrador, but nothing more. The brown manila envelope contained the news we would be flying the plane to Bari, Italy, and that we would proceed via Goose Bay, Simiutak Island, Greenland (call sign BW-3), Reykjavik, Iceland, Prestwick, Scotland, Valley, Wales, Marrakech, French Morocco and finally Tunis, Tunisia. The itinerary was flexible and subject to weather complications, but it sounded like pretty heady stuff to us. Oh yes, we also read that we were assigned to the 15th Air Force, 2nd Bomb Group, 96th Squadron at Foggia, Italy. It was very exciting, especially to me, 20 years old and anticipating adventure, real adventure, with our lives on the line.

It was soon apparent on the first leg of our flight that we weren't going to make Goose Bay because of weather. Checking the weather further it appeared that Presque Isle, Maine would be the logical alternate. Of course it was also socked in pretty good, and neither Archie nor I had ever shot an instrument approach other than simulated in training. I had always enjoyed instrument flying in training and Archie let me shoot the approach. It was a piece of cake and we were soon on the ground safe and sound at the Presque Isle Airport. As we exited the plane I'll never forget the local chief mechanic giving us a big hello. They had not been expecting us as most of the planes bound for the European Theatre went straight to Goose Bay.

At any rate, the mechanic made a startling proposition. He stated there was an abundance of young ladies working on the base, far outnumbering the men and that if we would like he could arrange nine young ladies for us to take dancing that evening. It didn't take us long to take him up on it and the nine of us, after cleaning up and dressing in our best uniforms reported to the rendezvous point, the Officer's Club. Sure enough, in a few minutes in walked nine real fine looking young ladies. It was unbelievable that anyone, anywhere, could arrange blind dates for nine guys and have them all show up without a "turkey" in the bunch. That event was a highlight, or at least a remarkable point in my life—something to remember. I don't remember the name of my date. You can imagine how she was selected. There were nine of them standing in front of us so I just grabbed the hand of the best looking one, at least in my opinion, and the others on the crew did likewise. Everyone was very happy about their selections and a fine time was had by all at a local dance hall. I corresponded with my "date" for months thereafter, but alas, never saw her again.

The next morning we were off the ground and tracking for Labrador. It was a good flight all the way, but the landing was interesting—on ice. The snow on each side of the runway was piled higher than our B-17. I made an interesting purchase at the PX at Goose Bay—a fur-trimmed cold weather hat with fold-down ear muffs. It was to remain with me for years and was especially useful in combat where I wore it under my flak helmet for extra protection.

After a couple of days at Goose Bay and a thorough briefing about the next leg of the flight, we were off one bright morning for Simiutak Island, Greenland. The station at Simiutak, commonly referred to as Bluie West 3 (BW-3), was a major wartime radio communications and meteorological facility on the southwest coast of Greenland and marked the entrance to the fjords that led to Narsartsuag and Julianehaab.

The approach to our next landing was very interesting. After arriving over the Greenland continent it was necessary to fly up a Fjord, past a sunken ship, turn a corner to the left and land uphill toward a glacier at the far end of the runway. Very exciting, but the weather was good and there was no problem. That is until we were taking off the next morning. Heading back downhill, of course I noted the air speed indicator was not working. A quick visual check revealed that the pitot tube cover had not been removed prior to the takeoff run. The pitot tube is the entry point for outside air that measures the difference in pressure—giving us our airspeed. The question now was, should we return and land to take the cover off or try something in the air. We elected to try to get the cover off in the air and continued on course. The first thing we'd learned to try in training for this situation was to try burning it off with pitot heat, normally used to burn off ice. That didn't work, so as we were climbing out over the ice cap we had our flight engineer hook the cover off with a piece of wire someone had found in the plane. Thus we got our airspeed indicator back in operation, which was a good thing because we were in for big trouble.

The trouble was in the form of a weather front that at the time of our departure was hanging over Iceland, but which was supposed to dissipate or move on by the time of our arrival. It didn't. Visibility was still zero at Reykjavik when we arrived. There were several airplanes that had left Greenland about the time we did, all bound for Reykjavik and we all wound up in a "stack" over the Reykjavik low frequency radio range waiting for the weather to come up to landing minimums. We circled, waited and waited, but the weather just sat there, zero-zero. We started getting low on fuel and the controller told us to shoot an approach in spite of the weather as we had no place else to go.

Now, this was the second instrument approach I had ever done and the first one at night—a night I'll never forget. The first totally blind approach right down to the ground revealed nothing but a one second glimpse of some wet runways and I had to go back to the radio station (cone of silence) and start the approach procedure over again. Meanwhile the airplanes above us were waiting and also running low on fuel. We were lucky to be the first plane in the stack because we at least had the best chance not to run out of fuel—if we could find the runway.

The second approach was interesting because we saw a little more of the field through the rain and darkness and searchlights burning brightly—lights that were normally used to spot enemy planes and I still don't know why they had them burning that night. They were a very real detriment to our chance of seeing the runway when they blinded us as they shone directly into the cockpit. However, on that second approach I can still hear one of the gunners call on the intercom, "We just missed the tower."

And the tower calling, "Dollish How, Dollish How, you almost wiped out the tower—you are cleared to land on any runway."

(Our code name for the flight to Italy was "Dollish How.")

Back to the cone of silence and back toward the field we turned, almost out of fuel with all the other planes in the stack above us waiting, also low on fuel. Well, on this third attempt the Lord was with us because the weather raised just enough to see a runway in time to land. Archie, who had been doing nothing in the left seat except sweating, took over on a half mile final and landed the airplane. I still remember that fur cap I had bought in Greenland which I was wearing with sweat streaming down my face but too busy to take it off, and Archie sitting over there in the pilot's seat, sweating.

When we got out of the plane, I noticed my right shoe string was untied. I tried to put my foot up on the jeep that had come to meet us but my foot was shaking so much I had difficulty doing it. That night we were told several airplanes did not get in and crashed nearby. Our radio operator, Sergeant Brodsko, came to our room and said, "Thanks, Frank. You saved us tonight."

I have to admit it felt good. I guess right there my feud with Archie really developed, because I had seen how incompetent, again in my opinion, he was. He could not fly instruments, period, and he was inclined to be very nervous in the clutch situations—of which we were going to experience quite a few in the next several months.

The next leg of the trip was supposed to terminate at Prestwick, Scotland. But because of bad weather at Prestwick we diverted to Valley, Wales instead. It was no big deal, not like Reykjavik.

Valley, a village near Holyhead in the northwest of Anglesey, North Wales with a population under two thousand souls, was interesting for us Americans, especially the warm English ale at the pub (actually cellar temperature, but warm to us) and the English plumbing—but definitely not the Welsh girls as they all had bad teeth.

After Valley, Wales, we were off for Africa and Marrakesh in French Morocco. We spent a few days there, enough to experience the fantastic heat in the middle of the day and the Arab natives with the big knives for sale. Our orders called for a direct flight to Tunis, but at the operation shack on departure an Army Major asked us to take his girlfriend, a French nurse, to Algiers.

We told him, "But sir, our orders read for us to go directly to Tunis."

He replied, "Just develop a rough mag over Algiers and land. Don't worry about it."

So off we went, developed the "rough" mag over Algiers and landed. On the way there we had a great time with the French nurse, letting her sit in my seat, etc. At Algiers, we decided to have a night on the town and hitched a ride into the city. We started out at a very dimly lit night club and managed to get very well oiled. Prostitutes were crawling all over the place and Brodsko, the radio operator, and I followed two of them at a suggested discreet distance—their suggestion—into a very dimly lit part of town. They had us exhibit our money on the way to make sure we weren't going to freeload. It was the middle of the night and my 1911 Colt 45 automatic pistol in the shoulder holster felt very comforting. With some trepidation, youngsters as we were, up some dimly lit stairs we climbed, to be met at the top by a very sweet old French Madame. Again, the Colt felt very good when some swarthy foreigners were seen in the foyer. Brodsko went down the hall with the chubby one—I believe I got it straight with him from the start that she was all his—and I went to another room with my choice. She was the better looking one, but not what you would call "classy." She was impressed by the Colt 45 when I took off my jacket and the extra banter seemed to jar my youthful exuberance because at this point my common sense seeped through all the rot gut I'd been drinking and I remembered all those warnings we had been given regarding the dreaded V.D. Quickly I told her I had left my betrothed at home and could not be unfaithful. I did, however, pay her the agreed price of $20.00 to avoid a ruckus. Damned if after the payment she still wanted sex. This surprised me from such a pro. Well, I told her I would cooperate, but not without a condom which I didn't have on me. Whereupon she disappeared for a minute, came back with the necessary equipment and we copulated like jackrabbits. Afterwards when I went into the hallway, Brodsko's fat beauty was running to the bathroom which was down the hallway. She was naked and the Madame chastised her for her nakedness—apparently against the house rules. Well, Brodsko kept his girl busy for a period after I was finished and worrying all the time about the V.D. which didn't seem to be bothering him in the least. By the time we left the house with a request from the Madame to be sure to come back, it must have been 2 or 3 a.m. We had trouble finding our way back to the Base in the wee small hours of the morning, even hitching rides in British trucks which seemed to be the only ones passing through town at that time of night. I remember walking through the countryside, passing Arabs with their big knives lashed to their belts, feeling the security of that Colt 45 again. By some miracle reserved for naïve youngsters in uniform we found our base out in the country.

The next day was "worry day" for Brodsko and me, concerned about whether we had contracted some dreaded V.D. Brodsko should have been worrying more than I because he used no protection and for several days we worried about V.D. every time we urinated. We lucked out, but the experience of worrying about V.D. cured me for whorehouses—almost. It was not until thirty years later in Central America that, as the result of booze and desire for some beautiful young Costa Rican girls, that I succumbed a second time—but now with a condom for protection.

After a couple of day's rest from our big night, we managed to fly on to Tunis and then on to Bari, Italy, our destination.

In Bari I had another interesting experience. "Reckless Ray"

Huckstead, our flight engineer got roaring drunk and started threatening other enlisted men in his tent with a pistol. One of the gunners came to our tent for help and I went with him back to Huckstead's tent. Upon sticking my head through the flap of the tent I saw Huckstead on a cot in a far corner waving his Colt .45 in a menacing way. I asked him to give it to me, but he just kept on waving it. Whereupon I just walked directly to him with the .45 pointed at my belly, reached out deliberately, grasped the barrel and took it from him. That was the end of that, but the experience stands out in my memory.

Just proves my present truth that there is nothing wrong with drinking, except it just destroys one's judgment.

In a day or two a plane from our new outfit, the 96th Squadron of the 2nd Bomb Group arrived to take us to Amendola Air Base where our outfit was based. I'll never forget how my heart felt when I saw that airplane. It was covered with patches from nose to tail from the flak hits it had taken and was really grimy with a thick coating of Italian mud on the bottom.

Amendola was a part of the Foggia Airfield Complex, a series of military airfields located within a twenty-five mile radius of Foggia. We were in the Province of Foggia, Puglia, Italy. Amendola had been repaired by Army Corps of Engineers in September 1943 and was put into use immediately by the 2d Bombardment Group of B-17 Flying Fortresses.

When we got to Foggia we saw that the other combat B-17's looked the same, in apparent states of disrepair. Actually, the ground crews worked at night to repair the damage done from the day's missions and kept the planes in good mechanical condition. They just didn't bother to clean the bellies, because the next take-off after cleaning would have covered them with mud again, mud that flew up through the holes in the steel landing mats.

We were taken to our assigned tent some few miles from the Amendola airfield. There was one occupant of our tent when we got there, the only one remaining from the prior crew. I can still see him sitting there. He told us his name was Pearl and that he was the sole survivor of his crew. The rest had been killed a month or so earlier during a raid on the Ploesti oil fields. He told horror story after horror story about combat flying and got us all really scared. However, I thought at the time that he was to some extent just putting on a show for us.

But after we had flown a mission or two I knew he hadn't been kidding us about the dangers of flying into Austria and Germany on daylight raids which is the way all of our missions were flown. The British flew only night missions, also out of Amendola airfield that we shared with them. As we returned from our daylight raids they would be going out in their Lancaster bombers for night missions, one at a time since they did not do formation bombing.

## Chapter 7

# MY FIRST COMBAT MISSION

There was a 1:30 a.m. wake up call, a walk up to the officer's club for breakfast and then to the Group headquarters briefing room for the mission briefing. The day of my first mission arrived. Assigned to fly tail gunner for the lead ship—which was standard procedure for new pilots on their first mission— I could observe the Group formation from the lead ship and learn the ropes.

When we first entered the briefing room for our briefing there was a map at the front covered with a sheet. When everyone was seated and after pulling the sheet off the map to show us the target for the day, the C.O. started the session with a little talk. Then the intelligence officer took over to tell us what the flak coverage was supposed to be based on reports received from our spies in the enemy country. The anticipated flak intensity reported by our intelligence people was frequently in error—usually on the light side.

After the briefing we were issued escape kits in case we were shot down behind enemy lines, a stark reminder that this was for real, then loaded into trucks with canvas tops and benches along the sides for the trip to the airfield. It was a quiet ride, one full of anticipation and fear that it may be the last dawn we would ever see in our young lives. No glamour here whatsoever, just reality and fear that could definitely be felt in the truck on the ride to the field—thick enough to cut with a knife. Funny thing, it was that way on the first ride to the field for my first mission and it was still there on the ride to the field for my last one.

## Twenty-Five Thousand Feet Over Innsbruck, Austria

As our bombers passed over the initial point (IP), the start of the bomb run, the bombardier got his Norden bomb sight all set for dropping the bombs directly on the target. No matter what there was in front of the airplane in the way of anti-aircraft fire we were required to fly straight and level to the target. It was risky business and hard on the nerves.

That first bomb run into the target at Innsbruck started easily enough. I was back in the tail of the plane in the tiny, tiny space allotted to the tail gunner who was usually a very small fellow— which I was not. I had only been in the tail of a B-17 a few times in training and it felt extremely cramped and strange. We got the order to test fire the twin 50 caliber machine guns on the way down the bomb run, which I managed to do okay. I kept looking out the tiny window back there, looking for the flak which I had never seen before. Suddenly some black looking puffs were going by the tail. My heart pounded and my senses keened. But on second look it wasn't flak at all. The black puffs were "nickels," the propaganda leaflets we usually dropped on each mission for the benefit of the civilian population.

Being in the tail of the lead ship I had an excellent view of the mission. Occasionally our co-pilot, Colonel John W. Collens, would ask me on the interphone how the other squadrons in our Group were looking as far as positioning was concerned.

Then all hell broke loose.

Terrible looking dark black bursts with fire in the center surrounded by black smoke began exploding throughout the formation.

The flak got closer, the noise of the shells bursting very loud.

I smelled the gunpowder and saw the fire in the center of the bursts as the tail of the aircraft swung wildly back and forth, slapped by the concussion of the nearby shells.

Holes started appearing all around me.

I was scared.

Someone was hit in the front portion of our plane.

There was a lot of screaming on the interphone and I thought, *My God, if this is the discipline in the lead ship, supposedly the most experienced and best men we have, what is it like in the other ships?*

(As it turned out, a crewman had received a slight wound and was treated in the airplane with no after effects I know of.)

There was a small piece of armor plate just below my guns in the tail of the aircraft and I curled myself into a little ball behind that armor—as small as it was. It was my private "foxhole,"—or the most reasonable facsimile thereof in sight.

Right behind me a huge hole opened up after a particularly sharp jolt. I can still see it all these decades later. Pieces of spent flak, were flying all around me then falling to the deck of the plane. They were jagged pieces of steel of varying sizes, any one of them with death written on it for me.

Finally, and it seemed like an eternity, we got to the target, and the bombardier dropped the bombs. The plane suddenly lurched skyward, a few feet higher in the air from the loss of the bomb load.

Our pilot started evasive action, constantly changing course and altitude to confuse the aim of the flak gunners. The German guns were radar controlled and we were told they could pick which wing they wanted to blow off a P-38 at 30,000 feet if we didn't jam their radar with our special top secret jamming transmitters or overwhelm it with "chaff"—small bits of metal looking like Christmas tinsel that the gunners would throw out.

Toward the end of the war, at the time of my first mission in December 1944, the Germans developed "Window" to see through our jamming and the flak suddenly got a lot more accurate and deadly.

The short story is that after my first mission I returned to Base in one piece. The same trucks took us back to the headquarters building for debriefing. This consisted of the intelligence officer querying each of us about the mission, the intensity of the enemy fire and anything that would increase their knowledge of the enemy and his actions. It was great to get that over with, so we could go over to the Red Cross tent and collect the big shot of whiskey which we were awarded at the completion of each mission. Of course, booze was rationed to us—one-fifth a month as I recall—but that shot after the missions was most appreciated. Oh, they had coffee and doughnuts too, but the booze came first.

## Housekeeping

We were assigned to a standard service tent and it wasn't very adequate protection from the Italian winter rains, so soon after we arrived at the Foggia base we decided to build a "house."

We found Italian artisans who pitched in to help us build the walls from cement blocks and then mount a canvas tent top as the roof. We used transparent plastic for windows and it was a much cozier place to live than a straight tent.

Then we found an airplane wing tank to put up on a stand next to the house to hold the fuel for a stove—a steel barrel cut in half. An airplane fuel line went from the wing tank outside through the cement floor and up into the barrel in the middle of the house. The burner was just a piece of copper tubing with some holes punched in it and the fuel was 130 octane aviation gasoline. You can readily imagine that the operation of that stove was nothing short of exciting.

First, it was necessary to light it. We would let a little of the fuel run through the line on to the bottom of the barrel and then we would stand way back and toss a match into the stove. There was usually a small explosion as the fuel ignited, at which time we would crack the valve to allow a very small amount of the high octane aviation fuel to continue through the burner. The stove would actually roar with that high test gas being burned, turn cherry red, including the stove pipe all the way to the top of the tent. It really kept the place warm.

Most of the other tents had similar set-ups and it seemed like at least one burned down every week. That created further excitement, because we all kept ammunition in the tents and it would be exploding while the tent was burning, causing everyone to take cover. After a while we were ordered to remove all ammo from the tents.

One feature of the tent area still stands out in my memory. Within each block there were four inch pipes stuck in the ground at a proper angle and right out in the open. These were "relief tubes" into which we urinated. It was very handy, but a bit embarrassing if a lady would walk through the area—such as on one occasion with Senator Margaret Chase Smith!

## *Risky Business*

The Battle Order was posted each evening on the Squadron Headquarters shack bulletin board, listing the names of the crews that would fly the next day. Needless to say it was carefully checked as soon as posted. Though we would not know the destination of the bombing mission until the next morning at briefing, we always hoped it would be a milk run to a target without much flak.

When I started flying my missions enemy fighter aircraft were not much of a problem because the German Luftwaffe was almost dead by December of 1944 and they only attacked stragglers. The flak, however, got heavier and more and more accurate as the war neared its conclusion. The Germans just got better with practice and more guns were available as they took their flak guns with them as they retreated on all fronts.

Climbing toward the target on each mission after crossing into enemy territory, an irritating noise would begin in our headphones that sounded like ten air raid sirens all pulsating in unison. The closer to the target, the higher we climbed, the louder the noise became. This was not only nerve-racking by itself, but also made ship to ship communication more difficult. It was created by the Germans "jamming" our communication frequencies. They were looking for just the effect it had on us and it really was an annoyance, but something we just learned to cope with.

One recurring problem for me was a burning sensation in my chest the higher we climbed and the closer we got to the target. The pain was centered in my left breast, over my heart. Finally, after six missions I decided to see the flight surgeon about it. By then I had become convinced I had a serious heart condition that was compounded by the higher altitudes. I went to the medical office with the problem after finding myself on the battle order for the next morning and described my symptoms to the flight surgeon in detail. He listened attentively and when I had finished he asked, "How many missions have you flown?" When I told him I had flown six and was on the battle order for the seventh in the morning, he replied, "Oh, you have the seventh mission problem." Without so much as thumping my chest, listening to my heart, taking my blood pressure, or for that matter looking at me with more than a sideways glance he went to the wash basin nearby and took down a large water glass tumbler and a bottle of bourbon. Pouring that glass to the brim with whiskey he came back to me, handed me the glass and said, "Drink this, all of it, right now, walk back to your tent, go to bed and everything will be fine in the morning."

I did as ordered, perhaps the first and last full glass of liquor I have ever consumed in chug-a-lug fashion (except for one I'll recount shortly). I walked directly to the tent, managed to get my clothes off and passed out on the cot. That was all she wrote for old Frank, as the next thing I remember was the wake-up person knocking on the door at 2 a.m. Strangely enough, I did not have a hang-over and there was no burning sensation in my chest as we climbed toward the target. That convinced me that my burning had merely been a state of nerves from having flown six missions—a nervous condition so commonly repeated that the flight surgeon, wise and experienced as he was, knew instantly what was wrong with me merely by learning the number of missions I had flown. So that was the end of my burning sensation and thoughts of going home for medical reasons. I now knew I was going to have to stay there and sweat it out—or go home in a pine box.

## *December 31, 1944—New Year's Eve*

I had saved a bottle of rationed whiskey with which to celebrate the New Year. It was raining outside the tent and for some insane reason I decided to get myself into a celebratory condition as fast as I could. Lifting the fifth of whiskey to my lips I drank and drank and drank. Perhaps I was trying an experiment to see if instantly downing a large quantity of booze—as I had for the flight surgeon—would produce the hang over-less result. What a fool I was!

After chugging down most of that fifth without stopping, until I could drink no more, I felt thirsty. Our water source was from a military water trailer ten yards from the tent door and I headed for it through the rain with my G.I. mess cup held high. I got to the water trailer okay, managed a few sips of water and started back for the tent door—I never made it. An overwhelming sense of nausea hit me and I lost all sense of equilibrium, collapsing into the Italian mud, unconscious.

How long I lay there I don't know, but one of my crew eventually came out looking for me and dragged or carried me into the tent, dumping me unceremoniously onto my cot. Believe me, I was one sick pilot the next morning and one that laid off booze for several days thereafter. Not for long, though, as it seemed I just lived for the times when I could get some drinking done—to forget the pickle we were in, just praying to stay alive as we flew down those flak-filled bomb runs to the targets.

As the war proceeded into 1945 the targets we hit became better and better protected by flak. Fortunately, though, the Luftwaffe continued to scramble only after stragglers out of our formation. By now they didn't have the fighter planes to risk attacking our large formations since flying close formation concentrated our fire power.

**Foreground: Our Water Supply at Amendola Air Base, Italy**
**Background: Our "Home" w/covered front entrance.**

**B-17 in flak over Vienna, Austria, on a bomb run.**

# Chapter 8

# BAPTISM OF FIRE

One morning at briefing we listened to an extra-long talk by the Colonel. It was my eighth mission. He announced that we were going to hit the last oil refinery the Germans had. It was the Ruhland Refinery a short distance south of Berlin and it would be protected, he said, by very heavy flak concentrations. Also, this would be the longest and highest mission flown in the European Theatre of operations and we would have to practice long range cruise control to the nth degree consistent with the need to climb with a full bomb load. He made a special point of stating that no pilot was to "scrub." (To scrub meant to cancel your flight for any reason. Reasons were usually mechanical, but occasionally problems were feigned by some pilots to avoid having to go to particularly dangerous, well-protected targets. Some pilots had a reputation for finding some mechanical reason to turn around and return to the base whenever the target was other than a milk-run.)

This target, he told us, was of prime importance to the war effort.

If we could knock it out we might win the war with a single stroke because there would be no more fuel for the German war machine. He was dramatic, emphasizing that some of us might not make it back. He talked a lot about crash strips that were set up to receive any of us that could not make it back all the way to our home air-field—Amendola. Well, I'll tell you there was a heavy feeling in the air that morning as we rode the truck to the airfield. Death, the fear of it that is, was evident in the silence—not too many jokes that day.

The route to Berlin took us near Prague, Czechoslovakia, the country of my forefathers. For fuel conservation reasons our climb that day was very gradual and our ultimate bombing altitude was very high – thirty-five thousand feet. That's as high as you could get a B-17 with a full bomb load. I was told it was the highest mission flown in the European Theatre during the entire War. I don't remember exactly how high we were as we passed Prague, but it was about twenty-five thousand feet. What I do remember is that we encountered some uncharted flak while we were climbing in the clouds and it was heavy and accurate. It was a prelude of things to come.

About the time we were coming out of the flak we lost most of the power on #1 engine—on the far left—and it was obvious that the turbocharger had failed. We had been instructed that the first thing to do in this situation is to have the radio operator pull the cover on the inverter buried in the radio room floor and check for a burned out tube. If it was burned out, we were told to use a penny to insert in place of the tube and it might suffice to bring the turbo back on line—it didn't work that day. To stay with the formation with just three engines, and with a full bomb load and climbing, it was necessary to over boost the three remaining engines into what was known as "war emergency power." We knew this would probably destroy the engines in a few minutes—unless one was very lucky indeed.

We definitely didn't want to drop out of formation while trying to solve the problem. Pilot Freebairn talked to radio operator Brodsko about checking the inverter while I over-boosted the remaining three engines to stay in formation.

Within a few minutes, when it was apparent we could not get the turbocharger back on line, Freebairn started sweating profusely, shaking and unable to communicate further with the crew. It was obvious that we had lost our erstwhile Airplane Commander. In a moment of decision—and self-preservation—it was apparent to me that I had best take over the aircraft and command of the crew. I had choices, hard choices to make. I could turn around and fly back to the base or continue to over boost the remaining three engines and stay in formation. We might even make it to the target with the bombs as we had been ordered to do. I can still feel the mike button under my hands as I announced to the crew, "We will continue on three engines in formation to the target. We will do it on three!"

Freebairn sort of bowed his head and shook while I continued to fly in formation, climbing toward the target. Within 50 miles or so of the I.P (Initial Point), we could see the flak ahead, and what a flak display it was. Turning my head to the left I could see that it extended from the I.P. for miles and miles all the way to the target—still some fifteen minutes ahead. This was different than anything we had been through before. Flak usually had lasted for only five or ten minutes at the most before and after the target. I turned at the I.P. to the left and into a wall of deadly enemy fire bursting all around. The blasts were exploding everywhere, especially straight ahead at our altitude. We just had to continue into it—we had to continue to fly straight and level so that the lead bombardier could get his Norden bomb sight zeroed in on the target.

Shortly into the bomb run the #3 engine, the one next to me

on the right wing, shook as flak hit a fuel line and I had to shut it down and feather the prop. Then #2, the engine on the inside of the left wing took a hit in an oil line and started streaming oil behind. Just then the lead ship in our squadron was severely damaged—I was flying on his left wing—and he dropped out of formation. This ship had the Squadron Commander aboard and as he was leaving he instructed us to salvo the bombs—drop them all at once. Problems continued to mount as the only ship with a real bombardier rather than just a toggelier was also hit and dropped out. This ship was the group leader with the C.O. of the 2nd Bomb Group aboard. By his command the other five ships in our Squadron salvoed their bombs.

Now I had only one good engine out of four and even after salvoing all bombs could no longer sustain level flight—my ship was going down! #1engine had no turbo charger so at that high altitude was just along "for the ride," #2 engine was leaking oil, #3 was feathered leaving #4 engine as the sole engine without a problem.

Up until this time I had been doing all the flying, as Freebairn was still in a state of shock from having to over-boost three engines for the last hour or so. But he came to life somewhat after we had salvoed the bombs and headed South. I really didn't know how far we could get with our damaged ship so I had a semblance of a discussion with him. Our choices were go to Russia or Switzerland or try to make it back to Foggia. We opted to try to make it home to Foggia nursing the damaged airplane along in a gradual descent.

Then a gunner called out, "Fighter at three o'clock high."

Looking to my right and up I saw my first German fighter in the ten missions I'd flown.

For some reason known only to God he or his unseen buddies did not jump on us and we continued south.

It soon became apparent that we were not going to make it all the way home as we were losing altitude too quickly. A study of the map revealed that there was a crash strip at Zara, on the Adriatic Sea south of Udine. We decided to land there. About the time we had the field in sight pilot Freebairn recovered enough to take over and land the damaged ship without incident.

We parked our ship amidst a bunch of wrecked airplanes then climbed out and took a look at it. I can still remember the last three numbers on our tail—395—the worst flying B-17 in the 96th Squadron. We did not bother to count the flak holes as we usually did after a mission. There were too many. It was riddled with holes, but miraculously none of us were hit. I can remember looking back once at old 395, and then just walking away without looking back again. I hoped I would never see that bugger again!

We stayed at the Zara emergency strip a couple of nights on reduced rations and amenities until a ship from our Group landed to take us back to our base. It was a C-45, and I remember it as a welcome sight. As soon as we got back to the base we were de-briefed by intelligence officers and I reported to the Operations Officer that Freebairn had gone comatose when we lost the #1 turbocharger over Prague and I had taken over as Airplane Commander, making the decision to attempt to complete the mission on three engines. The Operations Officer must have believed me—or confirmed with other crew members— because Freebairn never flew as 1st Pilot again.

Recently I've been able to confirm what happened to Freebairn as a result of my report to the Squadron Operations Officer about my taking over as airplane commander after loss of the turbocharger on #1 engine. All of our 2nd Bomb Group mission records are on the website of the Group. A check of our records confirmed that after the 15 March 1945 mission to Ruhland, Freebairn was demoted to co-pilot and never flew as 1st pilot again.

We were informed that since we had to land on the crash strip at Zara and didn't make it home with the plane, each of us had the option to take a week off at a rest camp. The entire crew opted to go to rest camp—except me and Brodsko, the radio operator. We made the decision to stay with the program in an effort to get our thirty-five missions flown so we could go home. Imagine our chagrin when we checked the battle order on the bulletin board that night and discovered our names to fly a mission the very next day. But that is only part of the story. Eight days later, after a couple of other missions elsewhere, when the C.O. uncovered the briefing map for our next mission my heart really skipped several beats—the target for the day was the Ruhland Oil Refinery!

## Another Face-off with Death

We listened to the "maximum effort speech" from the C.O. again the next morning—about how important it was to the war effort to knock out that refinery and that it was the last one the Germans had so that no planes were to turn around or scrub the mission at any time unless it was imperative.

Since 1st pilot Freebairn and the rest of the crew had gone to rest camp, I had been assigned to fly co-pilot for a pilot named John Reed. It soon became apparent that he was an excellent pilot, first class and quite a contrast to Freebairn. I should mention first, before getting into the mission, that on the ride to the airfield from the briefing, I was convinced that I would have to be very lucky to survive that day.

The flak on that last mission to Ruhland had been thicker than any we had encountered—absolutely murder. I was plum scared about what we'd see today. Everything went beautifully on the climb up to the target. Reed proved himself to be a fine formation pilot, sticking our plane right next to the wing of the plane we were flying on and holding it there in a very smooth fashion. He was a pleasure to fly with. When we got within visual range of the Initial Point (I.P.) there was flak at our altitude, 35,000 feet, and it stretched all the way to the target just as it had on the last mission. This time, however, we turned down "flak alley" without incident—other than collecting lots of flak holes in the airplane.

Deadly German shells were bursting all around us and the smell of gun powder filled the cabin. Much turbulence was created from the bursting of the powerful shells. When they were bursting dead ahead it was a temptation to just peel off and get the hell out of there—one to which we could not yield. That would be desertion under fire and was not given even passing consideration.

Close formation on the bomb run occupied our undivided attention, since the closer the formation the closer the bomb pattern on the target, especially important on this particular target as the last oil refinery the Germans were able to operate. In spite of the heavy and long-lasting flak, we made it to the target and the bombs were dropped on the target when our lead bombardier dropped his. We immediately went into evasive action with a left turn, changing our altitude as we did, down, to confuse the flak gunners. We were in the middle of that left turn when the tail gunner called on the intercom, "The right wing's on fire, I'm bailing out."

We were now over Berlin.

I looked out the right window and sure enough, there was black smoke pouring out the entire length of the wing. It looked like the smoke was centered around the #3 engine so I instantly replied, "Hold up a minute, we'll feather #3 and see if the fire will go out." At the same time I pulled the fire extinguisher on #3 engine. Reed was flying the airplane, staying in formation only briefly as we were getting no further help from #3 engine. When the prop finished turning to the feathered position the fire went out—miraculously from my point of view. Now we were rapidly losing the formation, not an appealing situation, since again we became a prime target for enemy fighters. We hadn't got hit by fighters the last time we lost the formation, but that was no assurance that we would not get jumped this time.

After a brief conference with Reed we decided to un-feather #3, try to start the engine and take a chance on the fire not starting up again. It was a real risk, but one that we had to do right away as it only would take about a minute and a half or so before the oil would congeal at that altitude in the extreme cold temperature of -40°C or so. We managed to get the prop turning, and the engine started perfectly. No more fire so we "poured the coal to it" and caught up to the formation. We flew all the way back to the base at Foggia from Berlin without incident.

When we landed and taxied to the hard stand, shut down and jumped out, we pulled the inspection plate on that right wing. When I looked up into the wing I was startled to see all of the ribs and other metal parts inside the wing were partially melted from the intense heat of the fire—the entire wing had been destroyed internally. Now, just how much longer that fire would have burned before all of those tanks with high test fuel remaining would have exploded I don't know—but that must have been the closest I've come to dying in the air before or since.

After the mission, both Brodsko and I decided perhaps we had better head for rest camp. I don't recall where he went as he was an enlisted man. Officers had different places to go. I went to Capri off the coast of Naples, a most delightful place. The Army had taken over a swank hotel that sat on the top of a steep hill overlooking the Mediterranean Sea. I remember I spent a good deal of time looking for some female companionship, but it didn't work out. One gal that had come to the hotel to play cards or something with the troops was, at my request, to take me to her house. She told me where to meet her ... a small house on a narrow alley. I stood there and waited for an hour before I accepted the fact that I had been stood up.

All good things must end and so did rest camp. So it was back to Foggia for some more combat. The war was turning very heavily in our favor in the spring of 1945, but the flak continued to get heavier as well. Every mission was still a matter of life or death. We just didn't know whether we would make it back from any of them. The ones we really liked were the "milk runs." Missions we knew at the outset before take-off from our intelligence reports that there were no flak emplacements. Sometimes this intelligence was inaccurate, but not as a general rule.

## *The End of the War*

Finally, when I had flown twenty-four missions, or "sorties," as they were officially referred to because of their long duration, the war ended.

If the war had continued and I had flown one more mission, my twenty-fifth, I would automatically have received the Distinguished Flying Cross and a promotion to Captain. But I can't reflect with too much remorse because that 25th might have had "my name on it" and all that followed would not be the history of my life.

What a celebration we had—yes, a drunk and rowdy celebration. Since I remembered my first attempt at drinking a full fifth of whiskey at one draught, I paced my imbibing so I didn't get sick—just hung-over. It didn't take long for our unit to be moved to a staging area to await further orders, hopefully back to the States. I remember that area well. We were in regular tents, no half house and half tent anymore like we had built at Foggia. Two events stand out in my memory especially. One was a buzzing B-17 that made me hit the ground as it passed at tent-top height. Just as it passed me it shuddered as it struck a power pole with its left wing and a wire wrapped around the wing tip. The trailing wire snagged an Italian boy who had been riding on top of a fuel truck going down the road by the tent area—he was killed instantly. The plane landed at a nearby base without incident and the pilot, we learned, was court-marshaled and received some prison time.

All pilots were guilty of buzzing occasionally. The trick was not to get too close or "over enthusiastic." I had learned that lesson while breaking in a new engine (slow-timing, we called it).

A new engine was run at reduced power settings in the air for about ten hours prior to being used on a mission. We used those opportunities to do sightseeing all over Italy. On one occasion we had flown over to Capri with the express idea of buzzing the officer's club on top of that hill where I had stayed at "rest camp." I was flying the airplane as we came up toward the top of the "saddle" where the club was located—flying close enough to the tile roof to blow a few tiles off. I then continued down the other side at roof-top level when suddenly the blue Mediterranean blended with the blue Italian sky and I completely lost my spatial orientation. I was in a steep right bank when the vertigo hit me and instantly went to the artificial horizon to get oriented. As I flattened out the bank the waves were licking the lower ball turret and the crew was rightly pissed off with me for almost killing everyone. That lesson has stayed with me throughout my life and I have never again tried to see how close I could come to anything with an airplane.

Later with helicopters, much later, 30 years later, I did a few foolish things, but not in an airplane.

The other incident in that tent area that has stayed with me is of an entirely different genre. A couple of Italian prostitutes visited the tent area and received a lot of patronage in an adjoining tent. I was too scared of V.D. to participate, but they found plenty of takers. They stood outside the tent which was the scene of their operations. A fellow poked his head in our tent and announced one of the gals was going to put on a show for all to enjoy. I went to the other tent but found it was too full of cheering soldiers to get in. By raising the side of the tent we managed to get in a position where we could watch the proceedings. Well, it turned out the show was going to consist of watching this kind-hearted pro being humped by a dog. A lucky canine was located, a spaniel type. She (The Pro) lay on her back on a blanket while a willing soldier lined up the dog between her legs, assisting the dog in his heated and frantic attempts to get it in. As I recall, the gal cried out in a pitiful voice, "I don't want to have puppies." With that little incident out of the way, I went back to my tent and ruminated about the depths of depravity into which boys can fall if they have time on their hands and are closely packed together as we were in that tent area.

One thing I accomplished while we were waiting for orders was applying for 1st pilot rating. I took a check ride as airplane commander (1st pilot) and passed with flying colors. At least I would be able to say in later years that I had been checked out as a first pilot prior to returning to the States. It's an embarrassment for me then that I have to relate that I was a co-pilot. It still hurts a little, but not much. I considered myself far superior to my original 1st pilot, Freebairn.

Oh, I had received a promotion to 2$^{nd}$ lieutenant just prior to going overseas, while Freebairn, the airplane commander, was still a flight officer—and about midway through my tour I was promoted to 1$^{st}$ lieutenant, just my final jab at him. At least it meant more money. As I recall, $200.00 base pay plus 50% for flight pay— $300.00 a month! What a deal!!!

# Chapter 9

# HOME AGAIN

I finally drew a co-pilot's position on a plane headed for the States. It was an interesting plane, one called at the time a "half and half" because it was the result of joining the rear end, starting right back of the trailing edge of the wing, with the front end of another plane. That way they could take two wrecks and sometimes come up with one good airplane. We had an uneventful trip home via the Azores and St. Johns, Newfoundland. After combat the weather we encountered on the way home was mere child's play as far as the excitement is concerned.

We weren't getting shot at.

We stopped at Fort Dix, New Jersey and the first thing I went for was to buy, of all things, some fresh milk. We had had nothing but powered milk since we left the States about seven months ago. Fresh milk was unbelievably good.

The war with Japan was still going at this time, so our thoughts were about that situation and that we would probably be sent to a place where we could transition into B-29's. They were the primary bomber in the Pacific Theatre of operations. First, however, we were going to get a leave to go home and tell some war stories and it wasn't long before we were on a train in a coach car—the interior of which looked like it had been made in the 1800's with wicker seats and kerosene lights. But we survived and after a day or two at Jefferson Barracks, Missouri for some kind of processing I managed to return to Maquoketa.

My "home" was with my dad. At this point in time my mother was re-married and living in Davenport, Iowa and I would borrow my dad's car and go down to see her. Since I had lived with my Aunt I had grown accustomed to thinking of her as my mother, really. There was nothing I could or wanted to do about it—that is just the way I felt. I loved my mother in some sort of way, but I just didn't like being around her for any length of time. For one thing she smoked and although I was smoking myself at the time I didn't like seeing my mother do it. Then, she was not a good housekeeper like my aunt. Maybe it was also because she was married to a laboring class man and I thought I was above that. After all, my dad was a lawyer and my uncle was a world famous cattleman. So I could see nothing exciting about my mother's lifestyle.

This was "wrong" on my part.

After all, the Third Commandment reads, "Honour thy mother and father." But I guess when one's mother and father are divorced it becomes difficult for a child not to favor one or the other and I always favored my father. This was emphasized for me through the years I spent with my aunt and uncle. My aunt was just a different type of person, one whom I became very attached to. It was almost as if she and my mother were rivals for my attention, and my aunt won.

While I was home on leave, the Japanese war ended. A local celebration was announced and we went to my dad's office that overlooked Main Street which was packed with celebrants. I guess it was the wildest party Maquoketa had ever experienced. Of course, the end of the War changed my plans as I received orders to proceed to Santa Ana, California for processing and discharge. That was great news for me because, if you recall, my Aunt Eva and Uncle Otto Battles had a ranch not far from there in the Santa Ynez valley.

They came down to the base in Santa Ana for a party at the Officer's Club and brought a distant relative, Helen Peppers and her husband, a Colonel in the Air Corps with a ground job—"ground pounder"— of some kind, and their daughter. The daughter was about my age and I tried to get well acquainted, but that didn't work out. We had a good time, though.

## *A Civilian Once More*

Discharged in the fall of 1945, I immediately went back to the University of Iowa to continue my education. I went straight to the Beta house to live, one of the first of the returning servicemen to arrive. It was like heaven, as there were many more girls than boys at that time. The guys that were there were mostly returned GI's. One great thing about it from my standpoint was the ability to go into a bar at any time and buy a beer. In Italy it had been strictly rationed and was always in short supply. I remember I used to think over there how great it would be (heaven) to have beer available any time one wanted one. I thought I would never get anything else done as that seemed to be one of the most important goals in life, to have beer available and be able to drink it at any time.

What a narrow-sighted outlook!

But it was the way I felt at that time.

Every weekend in those days was time to get drunk, starting with the "Thank God It's Friday Club." On Friday afternoon at one of the local taverns that catered to the students we would drink umpteen glasses of beer—at 10 cents a glass. If we didn't get too sick, we would go from there to the Beta House for supper, pretty drunk, and then continue afterwards with some hard liquor and a party with a girlfriend. And there were lots of girls.

My girl at that time was Dorothy Parker who lived in Webster City, Iowa. Actually, she had been a neighbor at Yakima and had watched me show off on my Indian pony, Babe. Her mother had married a close friend of my uncle who was the editor of the Aberdeen Angus Journal and they had moved to Webster City where the magazine was published. Dorothy and I had a stormy love affair. But she was torn between me and another friend, Woody, who was also from Webster City. I was pretty much her favorite (I thought wrongly); in fact her only first love for a while. Maybe the aura of the Air Corps pilot with the silver wings got to her. We had lots of fights, though, mostly about whether we should have sex— which she always won. Finally, she told me goodbye and it really got me to have a girl tell *me* goodbye. I was used to saying the first goodbye in the best tradition of "love 'em and leave 'em." After several attempts at saying goodbye to me, none of which sunk in, I was talking with her, pleading in the phone booth on the second floor of the Beta House one night. Even got to crying and telling her how much I loved her, etc., when a brother Beta, much younger than I, called to me in the booth, "Shut up, you dumb ass." or words to that effect. They (the words) stuck with me and sort of brought me to my senses. I remembered them later when similar situations arose at infrequent intervals. Stand-back, they said, and take a look at yourself, take a look at what you are doing. Does it meet the test of reasonableness? If not, chuck it into the wastebasket.

# Chapter 10

# DORRO VERSUS FRANCESCA

I neglected to mention a very important event that happened just before I left Santa Ana for Iowa City. My Aunt and Uncle invited me to visit a cattle-buying customer of theirs, Elisha E. Converse, at his ranch near Santa Paula, California. The real interests here were the daughters of Mr. Converse and all the nice things my aunt was telling me about them. In fact, she said one of them, two years younger than I, Dorro, was mentioned by Ling, her mother, as being "just right for Donald." That sort of stuck with me, so I was happy to accompany them. What I saw at the ranch was really out of this world for a young soldier. It was a beautiful hacienda-style house with swimming pool and tennis court. And when Dorro entered the living room, the first time I had seen her, coming down the steps in shorts and wearing the biggest, most beautiful smile I had ever seen, my heart skipped at least one beat. When we got into a ranch coupe for a short drive, her sister Dianna was behind the wheel and as I got in next to her,

Mr. Converse (known affectionately as Dooley) said, "Look out for the one in the middle."

That was Dorro.

I was impressed.

We made arrangements for me to accompany them to a show at the Biltmore Bowl, a sort of swank night-club type place in Los Angeles. The Converses were strict tee-totallers, but in a picture we have of the event someplace I noticed some booze on the table. If I had anything to do about it, there always was. Before I left for Iowa, I met Dorro in San Francisco and took her to the Clift Hotel for dinner. I can still remember the wine and the aura of love in the air. She put me on the ferry boat for Oakland so I could catch the train for Iowa.

We started corresponding and I certainly did look forward to the rose covered, scented—always scented—letters. She sent me a picture taken by one of the leading photographers of the day, Hurrell, and I proudly displayed it on my dresser in the Beta House, or wherever I went. I always considered her to be, on a scale of 1 to 10 of the gals of my acquaintance, No. 10. Even though I went with Dorothy and a variety of others later on, Dorro was always there at the top.

I worked on my uncle's Santa Ynez ranch in the summer of 1946, a year after getting home from Europe, and the trips to Santa Paula for dates with Dorro were the highlights. But about this time I met another gal that created the great dichotomy of my love life, Francesca Jensen. She was the daughter of one of my aunt's friends, very beautiful and half pure Castilian Spanish, the other half Danish. She was not only beautiful, but nice. A different type of gal than Dorro. Dorro was regal in bearing rather than soft like Francesca.

At the end of that first summer, though, I left my fraternity pin with Dorro. It did make us sort of informally engaged. But I corresponded with Francesca also and I was more than a little confused as to which one I should really get serious about. When I was with one she was it, and when I was with the other she was it.

A lot like life itself—always time for decision, and being confronted with difficult choices.

I finished liberal arts studies and commenced law school at Iowa in the middle of the year 1946. That of course became a consuming passion and the change of going out to California became a welcome rest.

The summer of 1947 was a happy time. I was able to go out with Dorro most every weekend. But when that didn't happen I always had Francesca who lived near Solvang, also in the Santa Ynez Valley (right below Rancho Cielo, which became the retreat for President Reagan.)

The fact that I didn't tell Dorro about Francesca and didn't tell Francesca about Dorro seemed eminently ethical at the time. All is fair in love and war, my aunt used to say! Besides, they both went out with others—I think. At any rate, by the end of the summer a difficulty arose with Dorro, mostly about a fellow named Charlie Ebright as I remember. I went down to Santa Paula to see her one weekend, Charlie unexpectedly showed up and she sent me packing.

I guess I never forgot that slight.

I was a jealous lover.

The matter came to a head when I visited her at her folk's cabin at Lake Tahoe and at the conclusion we had a big argument. I asked for my Beta pin back, which she readily gave to me. I didn't write any more to Dorro for most of the 1947-48 school year.

Francesca–yes, Dorro–no.

I studied law very hard and made the honor roll by being asked to write for the Iowa Law Review. I lived at the Law Commons, the law students' dormitory, until the start of the second semester and then rented a room at a private home where I thought I would have more privacy to study better. Of course, when I did party I did a pretty fair job of it. Much booze every weekend at least. I had bought my first car, a 1946 Chevy two-door. This was a bit of a prideful thing and I rented a garage for it to sit in most of the time and walked to classes. During this period the G.I. Bill paid my expenses and my dad was always generous with spending money. I tried not to ask him for more than I actually needed. During my Army Air Corps service, I had sent him my salary and he had deposited it in a bank for me. I bought the car with some of that money, but dad supplemented the G.I. Bill for my spending, or should I say, drinking money so that the savings from the service stayed intact. A fact that would help me out later on.

In May of 1948 I was looking out my window at some very blue sky which reminded me of the color of Dorro's eyes, and I knew that I had to renew my correspondence with her. She was more than a cut above any other gal I had ever been with. I should say also that she was a very proper girl and that all we did was some more or less light petting. Much different than the ones I went with at Iowa—except for Dorothy Parker who was also very proper.

It is an unadulterated fact that a man has more respect for a gal that doesn't give in to pre-marital sex.

No question about it.

I wrote to Dorro, apologized for not writing, and we were immediately lovers again, if only by mail. I was really looking forward to seeing her when law school let out that spring.

My aunt and uncle were in Iowa in the spring of 1948 and they decided to ride with me to California in my 1946 Chevy.

What a trip!

On the outskirts of Las Vegas there was a terrible noise and the engine quit us. A nearby garage, or rather a tiny service station diagnosed the trouble as a broken timing gear and was able to fix it.

We pressed on to California, and the ranch at Los Olivos in the Santa Ynez Valley.

That summer of 1948 was a busy one. The work on the ranch was the kind I had always enjoyed—working with cattle, riding horseback, irrigating and all the other chores there always are to do around a cattle ranch. Most every weekend I would drive my Chevy down to Santa Paula to see Dorro, or go out in nearby Solvang with Francesca. Along toward the end of the summer on a Saturday night, Dorro and I had a date, drank a little as usual and I managed to find a driveway into a citrus orchard on the way home. It was part of the Limionera Ranch near Dorro's father's citrus ranch. We smooched, (old word for kissed and hugged) pretty hot and heavy. Then on the spur of the moment and completely unrehearsed, I said to Dorro, "Will you marry me, I would be great insurance for you."

What I had in mind was that whatever happened to her I would look after her, be there in any event. And I really meant it with all my heart. She didn't give me an answer, but said she would think about it. I didn't even think about popping the question to her after that. Just completely forgot about it, because I figured that her silence meant a big "NO."

A couple of weeks later we were in Santa Maria at the Santa Barbara County Fair, where we had taken some of my uncle's cattle to show. Dorro's dad also had some show stock there, either cattle or horses, I don't recall which. At any rate I managed to suggest at a break in the show that we go downtown for a beer. I had always been good at figuring how to get a party started. It was just an ordinary Santa Maria bar and we sat up to it and ordered a couple of beers.

Suddenly and without warning, Dorro said, "You know that question you asked me about the other night? My answer is yes."

I had to think for more than a moment about what in the world she was talking about, but it didn't take more than a second or two. She was sitting on my left and I was just overwhelmed by the prospect of what she had just said. When it finally sunk in, I don't believe I had ever experienced such happiness. On the drive back to the ranch at Los Olivos, I was just about beside myself with joy.

Actually, I figured Dorro would make an unbelievably good wife. She was beautiful, intelligent, and rich, or at least her family was. I had hearkened back to something my dad had told me when I told him about Dorro. He had said, "That's great son, fall in love with a rich lady and don't let the money bother you one bit." Of course, it was not the money. She was also very smart, a Stanford graduate and beautiful and we seemed to get along just great. I remembered how on one occasion when she had come to my aunt's house after I hadn't seen her for a while—but had been seeing Francesca—how good it felt to once again be talking to Dorro.

She just seemed to be right for me. I was sure.

I wrote my dad about our plans. The wedding date was to be on our mutual birthday, September 7th. She had been born on the same day two years after to my birth. I considered this to be another omen that this marriage was made in heaven, by God. On my next trip to Lingdooley, it was somewhat formally arranged for me to meet Dooley by the pool to ask for Dorro's hand in marriage.

I remember it well.

I told him that I loved Dorro and then I asked him to give his permission for us to get married. Instead of replying directly at first, he asked, "Will you be able to take care of her?"

The emphasis was on the "take care of."

Without hesitating I replied, "I will do my best."

That seemed to satisfy him. I thought afterwards maybe he had suggested I furnish a financial statement, but obviously by giving his permission he negated that was what he had in mind.

We were engaged in early August and the wedding was set for September 7, which didn't leave a lot of time to get ready. I should have figured that there would be a large wedding, but I was not prepared for the gigantic event that followed.

Dorro's mother had died in the spring of 1948 of a malignant blood disease. She had been a truly fine lady— Lillian, known to everyone as "Ling" hence the name of the ranch "Lingdooley." She was of Australian extraction, her maiden name was Taylor of the Toowoomba, Queensland, Taylors, a prominent family there. Ling was an early campaigner for no smoking when smoking was the big thing to do. She had a large brass sign right over the fireplace in the living room proclaiming NO SMOKING and she meant it. Also, no booze was allowed in the house and they never partook of it—a far cry from me, drinking having been my favorite form of relaxation since first starting college, to say nothing of the increase in consumption with the combat flying in Italy. In spite of the differences, though, I was very impressed with Ling and she liked me. As a matter of fact, I understood from Dooley that before she died she indicated that I would make a good husband for Dorro. I always wondered how much this had to do with Dorro's answering YES. Since Dooley mentioned to me many times that Ling thought I was the one for Dorro, I really feel that it had a bearing on her answer. Dorro thought a tremendous lot of her father and it did please him that she was marrying someone that Ling knew.

Soon after we were engaged, Dorro asked me, "Does it matter that I don't really love you? I will still marry you, but I can't say that I really love you!"

This was news to me, but nothing I could not handle at the time. I told her that it did not matter, that my love would make up for everything and she would learn to love me. I sometimes wonder if that question of hers should have clued me in to what was going to happen.

Not long after learning that Dorro didn't really love me right then, but was willing to marry me anyhow, I had a date with Francesca to break the news to her. The date started out like all of the ones I had had with her—lots of fun. When I told her I was getting married to Dorro she was crushed. She made such a sincere demonstration of her high regard for me that I said, "To hell with it." and told her I would marry her instead.

Nothing like firm commitment.

At this point we made plans for me to go down to Lingdooley to break the news to Dorro. Francesca had to go to Berkeley where she was going to Cal to get registered for the fall quarter. However, she did say, "This is dangerous for me to let you go to Santa Paula by yourself."

Truer words were never spoken.

I went to Lingdooley to break the news to Dorro that the engagement was off and I got another surprise.

She was crushed.

When I asked her about her statement that she didn't really love me she said that was in the past. She said she did love me and wanted nothing more than to marry me!

I couldn't resist her. Again, nothing like firm commitment.

I said okay, I'll tell Francesca—talk about "waffling."

**L-R: Dick Smith, Dorro, FDS, maid of honor**

# Chapter 11

# SO DORRO IT WAS

This time I sent Francesca a telegram—not taking chances on a personal encounter. It got the job done, although she did phone me later when I was at my aunt's and told me that it was not possible to love two people at once. She wrote me a letter advancing the same theme, but it fell on my deaf ears. This time I was committed to Dorro and that was the end of it.

Until I reflected, after we had married.

Because of my limited finances, Dorro and I agreed that I would not buy her the traditional engagement ring. She very graciously stated that she would be more than satisfied with a plain gold band at the wedding ceremony. That was a relief to me for my meager savings from the Air Corps were going to be needed going to school. Also, we agreed that I would sell my Chevy and we would keep her DeSoto Coupe, a much better vehicle. The plans proceeded and before I knew it, it was the day before the wedding (only a month or so after the Santa Maria Fair). I called the florist in Santa Paula about a suitable bridal bouquet for Dorro and they suggested Stephanotis. I had no idea that the bill would be astronomical for the day, $50.00 or $60.00 dollars. We were married in the Santa Paula Episcopal Church by Reverend McDougal, a family friend. My best man was an old Air Corps buddy, Richard Smith. As Dick and I waited for the ceremony to begin in a small anteroom of the tiny church, I got the strangest feeling of entrapment. Dick kidded me that I still could run, but that was the last thing I wanted to do. Dorro and I were married in a beautiful ceremony to a full to overflowing church. The Converses had lots of friends and they were all there. I felt sort of overwhelmed by it all but managed to live through the large reception on the ranch lawn, cutting the cake with Dooley's Masonic sword, and all the pictures on the lawn and lots more in the ranch house. After the reception we put on street clothes and exited via a ranch car to the throwing of rice and on to a neighbor's house where our car was hidden, we thought. Phillip French, a friend of Dorro's, was there first but we managed with much spinning of tires to escape the marauders and started the trip to Las Vegas for our wedding night. We had reservations at the El Cortez Hotel, a far cry from the large places in Las Vegas these days. Before we got there, however, we managed to have a real argument about which road to take. We got a little lost.

Throughout our marriage, this matter of arguing about which way to turn on any kind of trip seemed to be repeated. I don't know why. I've never had the problem with anyone else.

Our marriage night was beautiful and we really did get acquainted. I should say at this point that I had promised Dorro that when we got married I would stop smoking.

I broke my promise.

What can I say?

I was just weak when it came to smoking in those days.

Now, today, I can't stand the stuff, but things were different for many years.

The next day we drove to Provo, Utah, and a strange thing happened. After we had made love, Dorro started crying uncontrollably. I wonder why, to this day. Perhaps it was because I had continued smoking. Perhaps it was because she was sorry we had married. Perhaps she thought now that it had been a mistake. Perhaps she was just suffering a big letdown from all the excitement, I don't know.

But it happened.

This, along with a lot of other things in my life will forever remain a mystery.

This is life—to fail to understand a lot of things and a lot of the failure to understand relating to our failure to communicate with each other, whether it be husband and wife, offspring or strangers.

We finally got to Iowa and first went to Maquoketa so Dorro could meet my father. I believe my dad was truly impressed. I don't believe Dorro was all that taken with my father, but she never had occasion to know him anyhow. He gave each of us a crisp new $100.00 bill for a wedding gift.

I neglected to mention that the gifts at our wedding had been lavish. I had never seen more anywhere, but then I was not used to going to big weddings, either.

We went to Iowa City to find an apartment. I had already made arrangements for Law School. It was a hot, muggy day in Iowa City, as it can easily get in early September. The available apartments were a far cry from what Dorro had been used to and we made a mutual decision that everything was just too grubby.

Not good enough for *us*.

We would take a honeymoon through Canada, back to the Pacific

Coast and I would transfer to Stanford Law School. It was already too late to get in to the fall quarter, but maybe I could make it for the second quarter.

## Stanford Law School

We had a great trip westward through Canada, and then down the coast to Palo Alto, California. I talked with the Stanford Director of Admissions, Sam Thurman, who was not too optimistic about my chances for admission to Stanford Law. Stanford ordinarily did not allow transfers in mid-year to an applicant who had already completed half of law school elsewhere. But I must have made a convincing case, because I was accepted for next quarter.

We went back to Lingdooley, where I went to work for Dooley until time for the next quarter to start at Stanford. At this time I began to develop a sensitivity about having nothing in comparison to the wealth of Dorro's family. In other words, I didn't want anyone to consider me to be a gigolo. I wanted with all my heart to be successful on my own, without regard to Dorro's having a wealthy family. This continued to be a problem for most of our marriage and until I had a lot bigger ranch than Dooley. When I made the conscious decision to marry Dorro rather than Francesca, it was on the strict basis that the only reason was that I loved Dorro truly more than Francesca without regard to comparative wealth.

Francesca's family owned a very valuable property, Rancho Vega, and she was a descendent of a very proud and prominent Santa Barbara County family, the De La Questas.

I always made it a point to work hard to make an economic success on my own. But I would be less than truthful if I did not admit that Dooley was always a great help to me, including loaning Dorro and I substantial sums of money—finally up to $200,000.00. That

$30,000.00 Dorro had when we got married, inherited from an aunt, was also a great assist.

In the early days of our marriage there seemed to be some distance between Dorro and I. We could have been closer and I longed for a warmer relationship. I gradually began to fantasize about Francesca and began to feel that my marriage to Dorro had been a mistake. This fantasy stayed with me for about 12 years until we moved to Oregon far from Francesca. About three years after Dorro and I were married Francesca married a graduate of Boalt Hall, the Law School of the University of California at Berkeley, and lived in Santa Barbara.

When the second quarter of the year started at Stanford, Dorro and I rented an apartment in Menlo Park and moved there in a horse trailer—which is the way we moved several times in those first years. We swept the trailers out first and thought nothing of it. The first place we rented was a one room apartment. Dorro had started getting morning sickness and discovered she was pregnant a month or so after we were married. In that first quarter at Stanford she was sick a lot of the time in the morning. As the date for delivery neared, she went to the ranch to have her baby close to her home.

I didn't think much about it at the time, but I did feel kind of let out of it. Having to stay at school all alone and do my own cooking was a problem for me. About the time the quarter ended, Dorro had the baby. I drove down the coast to Santa Barbara Cottage Hospital in a big hurry to see my new daughter. Dorro was somewhat embarrassed that Evangeline was born eight months and eight days after we were married. We had no inkling she was pregnant when we got married as we had not had sex until after we were engaged.

I couldn't believe the appearance of our child when I saw her through the maternity ward window. It had been a difficult birth and her head was quite the worse for wear, but that didn't last long. Soon she was a beautiful baby. At first, though, I thought she was ugly and was more than slightly embarrassed about the whole thing.

I worked for Dooley again in the summer of 1949 though I felt rather dependent working for my father-in-law. That was a completely phony reaction because I should have been proud to be doing it. I just ascribe this to immaturity—in spite of the combat experience—or perhaps just wrong thinking.

It is too bad that we have to spend so many years making mistakes before we hopefully get our value systems straight.

During late summer of 1949 I had a bad experience with a horse my uncle had given me. His name was Barbados and he had never been broken properly and was kind of a "poison bronc." He would buck unexpectedly and rear on his hind legs always with the sensation that he might go over backwards—not under control, as my old cow pony, Babe, used to do. Well, finally he did go over backwards with me when I was riding alone on a black top road, coming down with his full weight on my right ankle and smashing it. I lay in the ranch road where it happened for about ten minutes before Dooley came along and took me to the doctor's office in Santa Paula. The doctor cut my boot off and tried to set it to no avail. First they tried to pin it, but it was soon apparent that the bone was not knitting so they put me under general anesthesia and put it together with a stainless steel screw. That took care of it—with lots of pain. I recall vividly how I used to look forward to the pain shots.

So when we went back to Stanford that fall, my right leg was in a cast and Dooley helped us move. I can still see him unloading the horse trailer in front of the little duplex we had rented in Menlo Park on University Avenue. When we arrived at the house, Dooley was already in the process of unloading, sweating like a horse. He was a good scout about everything,.

Generally, I maintained my respect for him. Although there were times when my immaturity got the best of me and I would criticize him to Dorro. She was inclined to hold him up as a role model, which I resented. I felt he was less than honest sometimes, but aren't we all? But his generosity was overwhelming when it came to his children and sons-in-law. On balance, he was a remarkable man, ranking high in my book of good people.

That DeSoto really came in handy that fall, because it didn't have a clutch so I could drive it with my casted leg on the seat—"Fluid Drive" they called it in those days. I got permission to drive it right to the class rooms which were scattered around at the Stanford Campus. Those were the days before the completion of a Law School building. I found the school work at Stanford very challenging, to say the least. The average level of intelligence at a private school like Stanford is way above a public school such as the University of Iowa. I really had to tow-the-line to get by, especially before I had become familiar with the intricacies of California law as compared with Iowa. All of the basic courses, such as Contracts, Property and Criminal Law, I had at Iowa, so I had to re-learn the California law on those subjects on my own.

We always went home for Christmas to Lingdooley. It was almost sickening to see all the gifts lavished upon us, mostly by Dooley. It was a far cry from the meager Christmases I had grown up with where my mother sold cosmetics to earn what she could to give us some Christmas. Growing up we each got about three gifts, and they meant more to us than all of the lavish ones that were given at those Christmases at Lingdooley. Dooley can't be criticized for this, for he was truly generous to a fault.

In my final quarter at Stanford, I hit my stride academically. I got an A in what was generally considered to be the toughest course in law school, Future Interests taught by Lowell Turrentine, a fine law professor. I was certainly proud on Graduation day. Dooley was there. I was lucky to have my daughter Eva there too, now over a year old. Eva was named, of course, for my Aunt Evangeline. I tried to get my dad to come out from Iowa but in his later years he refused to travel more than a few miles out of town. A lot of it had to do with his health—he just didn't have the strength to travel. He was truly proud, though, I am sure, to have his son graduate from Stanford Law School, even then the leading school in the West.

# Chapter 12

# PASSING THE
# CALIFORNIA BAR

After graduation I had to knuckle under to study for the fall Bar exams, especially since those basic courses I had at Iowa had to be re-learned to be in accordance with California law. Dorro was always a good wife during those days, putting up with a lot, and not asking much. Since I was still going to school on the G.I. Bill, I did get a certain amount of military subsistence pay. But a lot of what we lived on came from Dorro's investments of the money which she had inherited from her aunt. I just tried to ignore this. It would have been better for me to recognize it and show my appreciation more to Dorro.

Again, it is too bad we have to waste so many years before we come closer to recognizing what is *truth*. Being human, we never achieve a complete understanding of the highly complex concept of truth as a reality.

Finally it was time to take the Bar Exam in San Francisco. We stayed at the old Canterbury Hotel, a favorite of Dooley's. The problem was that although I felt quite at home, having stayed there so often, I was so nervous about that three day exam that I couldn't sleep at all that first night. I managed somehow to get to the exam site, however, but not before telling Dorro to get in touch with a doctor friend we had there, Jack Evans, and get two kinds of pills—one kind to put me to sleep and another to wake me up during the day. She succeeded, and I had my sleeping pills and Dexedrine, the latter exceeding my fondest expectations. The second and third days, with the help of those drugs, went much better than the first. I typed the exam as we had the option to type or write it. I had an advantage with typed exams because I had always been able to type at high speed with a fair degree of accuracy—a hold-over from the days that Jimmy Wendel and I were on the typing team together ... with all those girls.

After the exam we went back to the ranch to work for Dooley and to await the results of the Bar Exam. It was a really tense period as I just didn't know if I passed, and neither did anyone else. Being an all essay-type exam, a lot depended on the grader one got, and what his particular personal idea was of a passing exam answer. Finally the letter came, before Christmas, and we learned the good news. We traveled to Los Angeles to be sworn in before the Supreme Court of California.

Then I became an unemployed attorney.

But not for long.

## *Griffin & Cardoza*

It was not long before we set out to change the unemployed part. First Dorro and I called upon a firm in Red Bluff, California, which didn't seem too promising. It was a one or two man practice and the head man seemed a bit of an egomaniac. I soon learned that this was almost a universal trait of an attorney worth his salt … seems to go with the territory.

The second office we called on, the offices in search of talent given us by the Stanford Placement Office, was in Modesto. The Law Office of Griffin & Cardoza.

John Griffin and I struck it off right away. He, smart man that he was, wanted to meet Dorro who was waiting across the street in our yellow Chrysler convertible (our pride and joy purchased with Dorro's money—as had all of our early possessions.) John was impressed with Dorro, as was most everyone. She always made a good impression.

A little cold, perhaps, but very beautiful in an outdoor way.

She was my ideal for beauty and had a real head on her shoulders.

We also talked with Tony Cardoza, John's partner, along with John Trimber, an employed attorney. I got the job and off we went back to the ranch to get the horse trailer loaded again. We might even have gotten a cattle truck into the act. Moving was so much easier in those days. We rented the house at 309 Ferguson, Modesto. Not much, but certainly the best we had to that date.

My starting salary was $400.00 per month, which was above average for a new graduate. John said they would not pay less, which sounded like the right attitude to me. The offices were at 1007 H Street, right on the edge of skid row and we had all the business from that area. The rule was payment in advance and I began to learn quickly under John's tutelage what the real world was like. He specialized in personal injury work and the mark of success, of course, was how big the jury verdicts were.

Tony had most of the Portuguese farmers' business lined up.

That was the way the clients were on a busy day—lined up down the hallway, with the waiting room full. I became John's right hand man (co-pilot again), carrying his briefcase so to speak, and doing all of the legal research for him, which he could care less about. We started to have some real success. First, we set a new record for jury verdicts in Merced County, the home town of C. Ray Robinson, one of the most successful attorneys in his field in the Valley. This was a big victory for John and for me. John had a way with juries. Law technicalities he could care less about, but he was a good student of human nature and appealed to human weaknesses to get the desired results. The verdict seems small today, $125,000.00, but it was the largest jury awarded at the time to a single Plaintiff in a personal injury case in Merced County.

After Merced John and I came back to Modesto and tried a case for Minnie Sisk before Judge Halleck—with success. It wasn't much of a case, a suit by a practical nurse for part of the Estate of a deceased patient. The evidence was very skimpy, and I had to argue some legal motions with all my heart and soul so we could stay in Court. John had me escort our poor little old practical nurse into Court before the jury each day, creating lots of sympathy, all we could muster. John loved to tell how this poor little lady had to assist the deceased with her bowel movements—by hand. Of course, he did admit she wore rubber gloves, but the jury got the message.

I need to mention that we had a blessed event in Modesto – the birth of our son, Douglas, without complication. He was a beautiful baby from the start – not like Eva had been at first, with her battered head. The doctor Dorro had in Modesto was named Dr. Sam, but I can't recall his last name. He always had a cigar in his mouth and I remember the ashes dropping on the baby's blanket. But Dorro thought he was great, which he was.

Toward the conclusion of the first year in Modesto, I had been eyeing a possible shift to Santa Barbara. Dooley knew an attorney there, Clarence Rogers, who was looking for a young attorney to hire. I went down there and talked to him. He had a delightful little office in the old Carrillo Adobe, a Santa Barbara landmark that was maintained by the Fleishman Foundation, which had the office next door in the same building.

Clarence was a trial lawyer. Born in 1900, his age was easy to remember. This was 1951, his age 51, and now I look back and realize he was a relatively young man, but he certainly seemed pretty senior to me at the time as I was only 27.

This just proves what John Griffin used to say, "Viewpoint depends on where you sit in church." When I told John that I was leaving him, he was highly upset, to say the least. He had grown fond of me, as his helper, I guess. I liked him too, but Santa Barbara, with its cool ocean breezes and that beautiful Carrillo Adobe looked too good to pass up. Besides, John's practice smacked somewhat as ambulance chasing, whereas things looked a lot more classy and respectable in Santa Barbara.

Besides, Aunt Eva and Uncle Otto's ranch was just 30 miles away in the Santa Ynez Valley.

# Chapter 13

# SANTA BARBARA

Dorro drove down to Santa Barbara by herself to look for a house while I stayed working in Modesto. She was successful in finding an interesting old place on the Ullman Estate grounds, a remodeled polo pony barn. It was large, much better than what we had in Modesto. There was room for me to build a corral for a couple of horses. We borrowed the trusty horse trailer again from Dooley, pulling it with the Chrysler and as Dorro drove the old Chevy I had bought to drive to the office. We had an uneventful trip.

We jumped right into the social whirl in Santa Barbara, of which there was plenty. I had always enjoyed martinis, but I really got into them pretty good in Santa Barbara, even at lunch. Clarence Rogers turned out to be a very tough taskmaster – better known, finally, as an egotistical trial lawyer. The relationship was one in which I was to be an employee for one year at the salary of $400.00 per month, and then at the end of a year to turn into a partnership arrangement.

At the end of a year he asked me to prepare the agreement, which

I did, with a 60-40% split of the net receipts, rather than the 2/3-1/3 division which he had earlier suggested. I was undoubtedly being overly greedy, but that was the way I saw it at the time. A day or two after I had submitted the supposed final draft with the increased percentage I was advocating, he told me he had changed his mind. I could have an office association, but he had decided against a partnership with anyone at that time. This was a blow like I had not received before. Not even during combat flying in Europe.

Funny how all those life and death experiences I had in Europe somehow faded into the background, and now I was so broken up about a simple business arrangement. But I went home and literally cried when I told Dorro. I somehow felt I had been betrayed by Clarence Rogers. Of course, it was his prerogative and I should not have taken it so much to heart. After all, it was no big deal. So from 1953 forward, I was on my own.

I didn't have a large practice, really just living from month to month. Dooley was my best client, along with the Memorial Cancer Foundation, which he had started with a $100,000.00 gift in memory of Dorro's mother. I was made secretary of the Foundation so I kept the monthly minutes and did the necessary legal work.

I continued as attorney for Cap Sherrill, Trustee in Bankruptcy for Canfield Enterprises. The bankruptcy had restaurants and hotels scattered throughout Santa Barbara County, and we ran them. The Corporation had been founded by a local attorney, Ted Canfield, who became involved in gambling with some notorious characters named William J. Graham and James C. McKay, of Reno. These fellows had both done time in Leavenworth, and were founders of the Bank Club Casino in Reno where they hired Bugsy Segal as a bouncer in the early days. They also founded Cal-Neva Lodge at

Lake Tahoe. They apparently had taken Ted to the cleaners, winding up with the fee title to the Barbara Hotel, one of the main assets of the Corporation. Ted wound up killing himself in his Santa Barbara home, a couple of doors from our house in Mission Canyon.

Cap Sherrill was a wonderful old character. A pilot in World War I, he had sustained some horrible injuries in a crash, including the loss of one leg, one eye sewed shut, and some big ugly scars on his face. He was one who could scare you on a dark night in an alley. But he was a fine gentleman, with much business experience, completely honest and a fabulous sense of humor. We managed to save the hotel for the bankrupt corporation. I was proud that I had done most of the work on this case, as we wound up getting a huge fee for those days, $10,000.00, which Clarence and I split.

## Adding Ranching to My Life

In 1954 I went into partnership with my Uncle Otto Battles in the purebred Angus business on his ranch next to Los Olivos in the Santa Ynez Valley. I was able to purchase a small place, 150 acres, across the road from my Uncle's house on Alamo Pintado Road, with a loan of $60,000.00 from Dooley. He made the loan for a ridiculously low rate of interest, 2%. My Uncle put up his ranch against ours and sold me a half interest in his Angus herd on credit.

The ranch, which we named Buttonwood because of the huge sycamore tree on it, had a small, no, tiny, yellow house on it, on a hillside. Dorro agreed that we should sell the Santa Barbara house and move to the ranch. Our daughter Christine had been born in 1952, the first year we lived in Santa Barbara. With three kids we were crowded in the yellow house and before long we had four as Mary was born in 1956.

I worked in Santa Barbara during the week and on the ranch on weekends. My Uncle was always rather resentful that I didn't spend more time at the ranch.

The partnership, in a word, was unsuccessful.

The purebred cattle business was in a slump, which it often is, and we had to start borrowing money, using his savings pass book for collateral, at the local Solvang bank. Finally I had enough of losing money and suffering Uncle Otto's resentment of my law practice. We had a big shouting argument about my being gone so much. Right then we decided to have a sale, disperse the cattle and close out the partnership. Our splitting was not without some rancor, but we had the dispersion sale at our ranch as planned. Actually our agreement was for me to exit prior to the sale at no obligation or profit, and the sale was for Otto's account since I had not paid for my half of the cattle.

I felt very left out of the sale, as I participated in name only.

After the close of the partnership Dorro and I had our own operation for about a year. In the meantime we put the place up for sale for $120,000.00. We had paid only $60,000.00 for it just two years before. We soon had it sold for $120,000.00 cash, and I thought the $60,000.00 profit was just a lot of money.

Much more money than I was able to make practicing law.

We moved into a big rented house with pool a few miles away and looked for another ranch in which to invest. It wasn't long before a place called Rancho Los Amoles (amole means soap weed in Spanish) was brought to my attention by Mr. Fred Brown, a local realtor. Dr. Anker Jensen owned the place. He was a dermatologist in Los Angeles. He offered the ranch to us at $250,000 for 550 acres and substantial buildings including three old houses—one of which was a landmark in that it was a big old frame house that had been there since the turn of the century. This figured out to just about half of the amount per acre that we had just received for the sale of Buttonwood, which joined the place on the west.

It didn't take a genius to figure out that it was a good deal.

We paid him the $50,000 down which we had made on Buttonwood and gave him a Note for $200,000 for the balance. This included all the furnishings in the houses, as well as the farm equipment, which was substantial. We collected more furniture than we really needed.

We now had 550 acres of prime Santa Ynez pasture and hay land, almost twice as much as my uncle, and even more than the 300 acres that Dooley had in citrus down at Santa Paula. We began to feel at that point like we were really ranchers. Rancho Los Amoles was a beautiful place and we enjoyed it immensely. At first I continued to commute to Santa Barbara for my law practice, but after a couple of years of that, in about 1958, I decided to lease another ranch from a former client, Mrs. Gertrude Duff, and really get in the cattle business. I continued to do a little legal work from the ranch, but not seriously. I bought calves in the fall weighing about 400 pounds and sold them when they were yearlings in the spring at about 750 pounds. Originally we had a small herd of commercial Angus cows which we had bought as calves also. We finally sold them as I figured we could make more with yearlings.

Actually, the operation from the beginning was a real estate maneuver as it could not be justified as a ranching investment. We were looking toward increase in the value of the real estate, which was rapidly going into subdivisions all around us.

I must say at this point that when Dorro first saw the place, she said, "Buy it." Later, when she first saw the Oxbow Ranch headquarters in Eastern Oregon, she also said, "Buy it."

But that is getting ahead of my story.

Dorro and I dreamt of owning a real commercial cow outfit, one that could run at least 1000 cows. I was constantly on the lookout for one which we could obtain when Los Amoles was sold. In the meantime I increased my efforts to sell Los Amoles. Finally, Elliott Bradley, a local realtor who had sold us Buttonwood Ranch, brought a gentleman named Fred Marlow around. Fred was a long-time developer from Orange County and really knew the subdivision business. He could see the potential and paid us $150,000 down on a total purchase price of $500,000—which wasn't bad since we had paid half that 2 ½ years earlier, using only $50,000.00 of our own money.

About that time Dooley's mother, Mary Converse died while living on a portion of Ranch Lomita in Ventura County near Camarillo. Dooley sold us the portion, about 50 acres that "Captain Mary" had owned for $150,000.

**FDS and Dorro Family Portrait 1957**
**L-R Dorro, Mary, FDS, Douglas, Christine and Evangeline.**
**While living on the Los Amoles Ranch, Santa Ynez, California**

## Chapter 14

# AUSTRALIA

At this point in our quest for a real cow outfit we decided to go to Australia, the land of Dorro's mother's birth, to look around. I will never forget the departure from Los Angeles in the DC-8, my first ride in a jet airplane. For a former B-17 bomber pilot it was really weird to fly in a machine with no propellers. Our flight was at the time the longest over-water flight in the world, about 5000 nautical miles to Papeete, Tahiti. We left the children behind.

We looked at a lot of country and stations (ranches) in Australia, but saw nothing that struck our fancy. It was very interesting to visit Toowoomba, the home town of Dorro's mother. We visited the Taylor homestead there, Clifford House, and the family cemetery plot where the relatives were buried. Traveling as far north as Brisbane, we didn't seriously consider buying any property.

## *Back Home*

When we returned to the U.S., I intensified my search for a real cow outfit, traveling extensively in the States of Nevada, Idaho, California, and Oregon.

We also got to see Montana, especially the Bitterroot Valley.

Hanging in our kitchen at Los Amoles there had been a picture of a ranch at the foot of some tall snow-capped mountains. I had contacted a realtor in Missoula about ranches, and we flew there to look at some.

One of the first places he showed us was the very same ranch that was depicted on our kitchen calendar!

We thought it was fate that had taken us there.

It was owned by Curtis Martin of Beau Donald Hereford cattle fame. He had a beautiful little operation, running about 150 cows. It was not the commercial cow outfit we were looking for, but it certainly struck our fancy. Curtis was a real trader. The first thing I knew we were close to making a deal for the ranch and purebred Herefords on the basis that I would buy the ranch for his price, about $250,000, and pay for the cattle over a period of time by transferring 10% of the bull calves we produced to him. I prepared a draft of our agreement and was ready to go to his lawyer's office to sign it, when we learned one of our children—whom we had left at Lake Tahoe with a baby sitter—was very ill. We just had to leave.

It was not long after we returned to Montana a few days later, that I was notified that someone had come along right after we left and bought the ranch from Curtis for cash.

That was one that got away. It was a good ranch, world famous for its beauty. All of the Great Northern Railroad calendars bore photos of this ranch on their covers.

## *Back in the Air*

While we were still at Los Amoles Ranch, I had renewed my interest in flying. At first I rented planes from Burt Bundy at Santa Barbara Flying Service, but then we decided that we should buy one of our own. Burt talked with a fellow in Salt Lake City about a Bonanza and made a deal on the phone to buy it if it was as represented when we looked at it for $12,000.

I bought airlines tickets and we were off to Salt Lake. The plane was beautiful and as represented. When we were filling out the purchase papers and I was about to write the check, I turned to the seller to verify the $12,000.00 price.

"No," he said. "I now have a buyer who will pay $12,500.00."

That he was going back on the deal he had made with Burt so incensed me that I told him "no thanks." Burt and I jumped the first plane for Los Angeles. When we were sitting on an outside bench at the L.A. Airport waiting for the Santa Barbara connection, I asked Burt what a brand new Piper Comanche 250 would cost. When he told me $19,500 it sounded like a whale of a lot more than the $12,500 the fellow had wanted for the Bonanza, but I wanted an airplane very badly, so I accepted Burt's offer.

It took a few days for him to arrange delivery of the airplane, but it wasn't long before we had the Comanche. Los Amoles was not sold yet, so Dorro's money was utilized for the purchase. This bothered me a little, but not enough to stop me wanting this plane.

I had re-caught the flying bug and it has been with me ever since.

Dorro decided that she should learn how to land the airplane, but enjoyed flying so much that she went on to get her private ticket in the Comanche, and then on for an instrument ticket as well. By the time we were looking for a real cow outfit, we were flying a Beech Twin Travelair. That is what we had flown to Montana.

## *Oregon*

Of all the states we searched, Oregon seemed to be the best place to look for what we wanted.

One day I noticed a ranch advertised in the Western Livestock Journal with "vast hay meadows." I phoned the number given, and a realtor named Walt Kittredge had the listing. When I learned the price was $1,000,000 I didn't go any further—though I did learn it was the Oxbow Ranch at Prairie City, Oregon, a ranch I had heard about from childhood since one of my uncle's best bull customers, Sherm Guttridge and his family, owned the ranch.

His father, "Bricktop" Guttridge (named for his red hair) had practically homesteaded the place and had put a big share of it together. Kittredge had some other ranches to look at and I flew up to Bend to have him show them to me. We looked at several, including one I liked a lot in Silvies Valley south of John Day, that Slim Shetke owned—the Silvies Valley Ranch. Shetke was a big game hunter and had one building filled with real big game trophies. While very impressive, it didn't look like the right ranch for us.

Finally one day as I was bouncing along with Walt Kittredge, who was usually half loaded with booze, he said, "There's one in the million dollar category that's for sale—the Oxbow over at Prairie City." I didn't tell him I'd known about the Oxbow just then, but by this time I was tired of looking at ranches I didn't like and I said, "Okay, let's look at it even though the price is out of my range."

In a few days we were at the Oxbow and Wes Clark, the long-time foreman was showing the place to us. I had been on the place once in my childhood with Uncle Otto and recognized the setting at the foot of Strawberry Mountain on the north side. The house was huge, about 10,000 sq. feet, with fifteen bedrooms including the five in the bunk house attached to the main house and ten bathrooms.

The ranch was everything I had ever dreamed of—but how do you buy a million dollar ranch with only $150,000 cash? I told Dorro about it anyhow and not long after I returned to Santa Ynez from the first trip, we flew the Travelair back up to Oregon. I made a low pass on the north side of the large ranch house by the headquarters and she turned to me and said, "buy it."

Well, that was enough for me. I felt the same way, but how to do it was the question. We started by talking to the bankers. The Connecticut Mutual Life Insurance Company was loaning on ranches a lot at the time and we talked to Don Dryer, the Connecticut Mutual loan man, about it. He said, after extended discussions, including one over martinis which I remember well, that if we were going to live on the ranch and really work at it he would recommend a $300,000 loan—enough for a down payment.

We went back to the ranch to see if we could get a tentative deal worked out, particularly a commitment to a firm price worked out with the owners, Phillips and Haggarty. This was a partnership composed of Hugh Phillips, his son, Bill Phillips, and Bob Haggarty. I offered them a total of $900,000 if they would carry back a $500,000 second mortgage. Bill Phillips said they had already refused that offer once, but that they would take $950,000. This was breath-taking business for me, because I had never dealt in such sums before. I talked it over with Walt, and he gave me some courage. So I told Bill that I would pay $950,000 provided finances could be worked out.

We were sitting in the office at the Oxbow when we were having these discussions, which are forever etched indelibly in my mind because it was a "go for broke" kind of transaction.

Dorro and I flew back to Portland to see if we could arrange some financing. We stayed at the "Eastern Oregon" Hotel in Portland, the Imperial. I could not sleep, trying to figure out just how we could make the deal with $150,000, when the price was $950,000. For starters, and since the place only had one thousand cows on it, we would need another $100,000 for five hundred more cows, and operating capital for a year—total borrowed money of about $1,000,000.

In the wee small hours of that morning, I had an idea. I grabbed for my legal tablet and started writing. If we added the Connecticut Mutual loan of $300,000 to our $150,000, it would give us $450,000 cash for a down payment. We would ask Phillips and Haggarty to take a Note secured by a Second mortgage for the balance to them of $500,000. That would put us in possession of the real estate and one thousand cows.

We would bank on selling our portion of Rancho Lomita during the next year for possibly as much as the balance owing on the second mortgage. If the sale during the coming year did not materialize, perhaps I could discount the Note I held from Fred Marlowe to make the first year's payment to Phillips and Haggarty. Marlowe still owed us about $150,000 and with a little luck I could sell our portion of Lomita for enough to generate equity to us of another $350,000—just the right amount to satisfy the second mortgage which had to be on a five year pay-out. Then we would borrow enough to stock the ranch plus operating capital from the Northwest Livestock PCA, in Portland. That would mean that the operation itself would only have to pay off the $175,000 loan. With a little more luck we could sell thirteen hundred calves at $100 per head for $130,000 gross, which would pay the operating expense of $75,000, with $55,000 left to apply on the PCA loan.

Now I knew this looked great on paper, but the catch was to convince first Phillips and Haggarty to take a second mortgage to secure a loan to us of $500,000. We flew to Lind, Washington, where they lived, landed at the small airport there and got in touch with Bill

Phillips. He came to the airport and we went to a small restaurant there in Lind and I made the pitch.

Prior to this trip we had gone to Santa Barbara and talked to Dooley about our plan. I asked him if he would go surety for us on the $500,000 note to Phillips and Haggarty. We were in Castagnola's Seafood Restaurant on the Santa Barbara water front when we talked to him. He had known about the Oxbow and its reputation, so he was impressed with the property. Without hesitation, he said he would go surety for us on the note. So when we talked to Bill Phillips in Lind, we had this additional security to offer. Bill went for the deal. So now all we had to do was to go back to Portland and convince the PCA that we could handle it. We talked to Jerry Herburger, the manager, about the deal. He said he would need some recommendations and references. He said further that from their standpoint the gamble for them in the deal was that I had never run a fifteen hundred head cow outfit. I asked my uncle and another old time cattleman, Glen Cornelius, with whom I had done business in Santa Ynez, to write the needed letters to the PCA.

Well, the PCA after getting the letters and running it by their loan committee, said they would back us. The next step was to go to Don Dryer and get the Connecticut Mutual loan. That proved to be quite a problem because the ranch had to be appraised, and Don was known to be more than somewhat dilatory. By "riding herd" on him, though hard at times, we managed to get the loan through, in spite of all the heavy borrowing that was being done. We went to John Day and used the attorney for Phillips and Haggarty, Gordon Wilson, to put the papers together to make the transaction work. That was an experience, since most attorneys even then would not undertake to represent both sides to a buy-sell transaction. The interests of buyer and seller are divergent, and there is really no ethical way it can be done. I have found though, with my legal background, it can be the best way to operate. The alternative, for each seller and buyer to have their own attorneys almost inevitably leads to a much larger legal bill, and the two attorneys wind up prolonging the whole process—often killing the deal as well.

We got the Oxbow deal through in record time, in spite of the complications and heavy borrowing. Including the $175,000 we needed for cows and operating capital, it was a $1,125,000 deal, and we were putting it together with only $150,000.

I thought this wasn't too bad, or more exactly, real good from the standpoint of leverage.

At the time I am writing this, in 2013, 53 years after the Oxbow deal, a deal like we made would never work. Insurance companies are no longer making ranch loans at a viable rate of interest and it is all one can do to pay the expenses of operation on a cow outfit from net income, let alone pay any interest on a cash flow basis.

## Early History of the Oxbow Ranch

One great motivator for me to stretch myself so thin to purchase the ranch was the long history of the incredible Oxbow. The earliest account I have of the place is a description of a horseback ride down from Fort Clatsop at Astoria, Oregon, to Fort Logan—which was located on the ranch. The historical record was made by a U.S. Cavalry Colonel named Reno. He told of riding up Strawberry Creek Valley and recounted it as "a most beautiful place in the shadow of Strawberry Mountain."

## The Early Homestead

The ranch now called Oxbow was homesteaded in the nineteenth century by Christopher Henney Guttridge—"Bricktop" Guttridge. Born in England in 1829, he was married to Mary Ellen Stephenson. His descendants held the ranch until its sale in 1941 to Mr. Ford Twaits. Twaits was a prominent contractor. Among his credits is the construction of the Pershing Square underground garage in San Francisco. Just as the Guttridge family, he was a good friend of Uncle Otto Battles.

Ownership passed from Twaits through three other Angus breeders: Roy Johnston, Paul Grafe and J.B. McCorkle (who purchased it on speculation, I believe.)

The Guttridge Ranch (Oxbow) was known for its purebred Angus cattle. This was established with the bulls purchased by Sherm Guttridge from Uncle Otto from his Rosemere Herd in Yakima. I remember well riding pastures as a boy with Sherm Guttridge. So you can see what a prize it was for me, years later, to purchase the ranch. Albeit I was pretty well leveraged since I bought it with only $150,000 on a $1.1 million deal—land, machinery, cattle AND the first year's operating capital.

The Oxbow Ranch

Prairie City, Oregon

*Chapter 15*

# THE OXBOW COW OUTFIT

In January of 1961, around the first of the month, I took a pickup and horse trailer with two horses in it, an Appaloosa named Cojo Cannella, and a quarter horse named Raleigh, to Prairie City from Santa Ynez. The escrow closed shortly after I arrived and I phoned Dorro, who was standing by, to oversee the loading of our furniture in a moving van.

There was plenty of snow on the ground and the feeding of the cattle was in full swing. I can't recall of anything that made me happier before or since than those first days on that ranch. It was just everything I had ever longed for. I loved the riding of the pastures, checking the cattle, and observing the feeding from the horse-drawn wagons, or bobsleds when there was snow on the ground—all going on beneath that beautiful Strawberry Mountain.

At times I was almost overwhelmed by the thought of owing so much money. But I always said to myself, "What the Hell, I came into this world with nothing, so if everything is lost I won't be any worse off." Then I would put my nose to the grindstone and work harder. It was pretty much dawn to dark every day, and then doing the office work at night until bedtime. We didn't stray far from that ranch the first year.

I had banked on selling our portion of Ranch Lomita to get the Phillips and Haggarty second mortgage lifted, so I had to make occasional trips to California working on deals on that ranch. These would be in the Travelair, at times flown at night. I made about six such trips on different deals, none of which worked out the first eleven months or so.

The winter months at the Oxbow started about January 1. They were exciting times because of the necessity to "doctor" the new calves for calf-hood diarrhea, also known as scours. It was a matter of two of us riding through the cattle each morning as the feeding was going on, roping the sick ones, and after administering the medicine, marking them in special crayon with the mark of the day. This would go on all morning, and sometimes into the afternoon.

The feeding crew was three men, two driving horse drawn wagons, and the foreman Wes Clark, and I doing the roping and doctoring. Occasionally, there was an extra man or two, especially in the later years when we had purebred cattle as well as the commercials. We gave the men a hot meal at the bunkhouse dining room in the winter time and we were usually through with the feeding and doctoring by noon.

Wes Clark had been on the ranch since childhood. He was truly a "bull of a man," very husky and strong in spite of a spinal fusion he had, the result of physically throwing a horse in anger that he was trying to shoe. He was a worker, usually seven days a week. I paid him $600.00 a month plus house, utilities, meat, milk, and gas for his pickup, which he used on ranch business. It was soon apparent to me that he was putting me through a sort of hazing test to find out if I could stand the pace, or maybe to just wear me out. I was with him from early morning to dark every day, because I had to learn the ranch and I didn't know any of the routine. I had ranched as a boy for my uncle and later on as I have been relating, but never on this scale. It was a learning experience.

At first I couldn't catch (rope) those sick calves without several tries. The ground covered with ice or snow, my hands wet and cold, the wind was blowing a good deal of the time, all made for just a terrible time trying to catch those calves. I had never roped much, but I liked the challenge and, after several weeks of missing, I pretty soon began to get the hang of it. The feeders were always on hand to witness all the roping, which put more pressure on me, the boss.

The crew that came with the ranch was sort of a motley crew, except for Wes Clark. It seemed that he delighted in bullying the men, and there had always been a big turn-over in help. I soon learned that one of them, Clark Pangborn, was drinking on the job. He was the first to go. Another one of the feeders got mad and quit. It was always something on that ranch, but I loved it.

I should add right here that I was unable to actually "see" the ranch before the purchase, because it was covered with a thick blanket of snow. I bought it strictly on reputation and responses to my inquiries with respect to production, not only from the owners, but also from knowledgeable cattlemen and the principal banker in the area, Herman Oliver.

Along in March we had to start branding the calves. This was a real work time, because in the first place the little calves didn't follow their mothers very well and it was always a challenge just to get the mothers and calves into the corral. Then they had to be separated, the calves from their mothers. We had a chute and dodge gate to do this and it worked very well.

The corrals had been laid out by an expert. Mr. Ford Twaits, a construction man, had owned the ranch for a number of years and had built lots of the buildings during the war out of redwood. Expense was no object to him. We reaped the rewards of his efforts and wealth and I often silently thanked him for it.

The branding worked best if we had a crew of about five, preferably six. Two to push the calves in the chute, one to brand and vaccinate, that was me, one to catch the heads and dehorn, one to catch the heels, and one to castrate the bull calves. We often got by with less, but if we had a full crew we could brand four hundred head in a day. At first we branded with a fire and a heavy branding iron, but it didn't take me long to convert to an electric iron. This was not only easier, but made a much better brand, especially after I started clipping the hip before applying the iron.

About April 15 on the average, we stopped feeding hay and turned the cattle out on spring pasture on what was historically called the "section" land, because the only description we had on the title to this land was by the section. We had to feed on the hay meadows, because the section land got too muddy to feed upon. In fact, Wes used to say, "It could mire a saddle blanket."

Before turning out on the spring range we had to go around all the fences. This was quite a task in itself. We used to "horseback it" with minimum fixing. Where we could not get the job done this way because of the poor condition of the fence, we would send someone out with a wagon and more equipment. In later years we had a horse drawn freighter wagon to drive and go around all the fences and this resulted in a much better job being done.

June 1 was turn-out time on the National Forest. We had two National Forest permits. One was on the Middle Fork of the John

Day River. This was the main one for four hundred cow/calf pairs "outside," and up to three hundred and fifty pairs inside on deeded meadows along the Middle Fork. Then we had a one hundred head Forest permit on the North Fork of the Malheur River in the opposite direction from the Middle Fork permit. All together there was about three weeks of trailing cattle in June each year.

This was real cowboy time, necessary to get all the horses shod and to line up about twenty extra riders to help take the cattle out to the Middle Fork. Actually, the North Fork permit was for what we called the "Kent" cattle. They carried a different brand, the $\sqrt{/}$ rather than the Oxbow $\cap$. The reason for the two brands was because the upper limit for one outfit to have on the National Forest in that area at the time was four hundred head—and we had that many on the Middle Fork alone. Also when we bought the place we had Dooley identified as the owner of the Kent place with just enough ground to furnish hay for the one hundred head, and then he had to run the Kent cows as well. Later we sold the Kent permit and bought the Kent land back from him. The North Fork permit was proving to be just too much work for the one hundred head of cattle compared to the benefit we were getting from it.

To get the cattle to the Middle Fork permit it was necessary to drive right through Prairie City, with all of its hard surfaced streets, houses, dogs, children, etc. Range cows such as we had did not appreciate this very much. The only way we could make it work was to start driving from the ranch at "first light" about three miles outside the town limits where the hard surfaced streets began. With lots of help we would divide never more than four hundred pairs up into several consecutive groups.

The "leads," which I usually took, were only about twelve cows. This was so the lead cows could be controlled, because if they ever turned around or went the wrong way, the entire mob of cattle would follow them. The calves usually quickly gravitated to the rear, which we called the "drags," and it was here that Wes and his dogs were used to good advantage—as long as the dogs didn't start barking.

Actually, dogs in the spring are more nuisance than help. They get the cows worrying too much about the small calves and can make things go straight to hell. But when we hit that town with eight hundred head of cattle, including the calves, all hell sometimes broke loose in spite of anything we could do. If that happened we'd wind up making wild rides through fences, gardens, lawns, porches—whatever stood in our path.

It is not hard to understand why the lawns in Prairie City became well fenced.

After about an hour of getting through town, it was up the highway to the top of Dooley Mountain. We rested the cattle half-way to the top, about twelve miles, then again at the top. Eventually we were able to buy forty acres at the top of Dooley Mountain (we named it "Tip Top"), making it a great catch pen during the fall gather, a place to load after we built a loading chute, and a place to spend the night on the way home in the fall.

On the way to the range in the spring, we rested up real good for about thirty minutes at the top, because the next few miles were through the pine trees more or less on the level for about three miles, then a taking a hard right turn down a very steep and narrow trail dubbed "Monkey's Run." Named for good reason as only a monkey could handle its steepness and roughness very well—or at least a monkey would be the best type of animal to use it.

Monkey's Run wound up at the bottom on Placer Creek where we had some corrals to hold the cattle for the next day's drive. If it was a herd of the "inside cattle"—those summering on deeded ground along the river they were held here. But if it was a herd of the "outside cattle" we would just hold them there until they "mothered up" and then let them go. After that we'd leave for home.

Sometimes the leads would get to the Placer Creek corrals two hours before the drags would arrive. I liked to put one of our kids (usually Eva, a real cow gal) in front of the leads down Monkey's Run to hold the cattle back from running too fast. Sometimes this worked, and sometimes it caused a group to pile up or plunge off the side of the trail down into the bottom of the draw far below into very dense brush, where we had real trouble getting them out. It usually meant somehow driving them downhill at the bottom of the draw through the very dense brush, on foot, leading your horse.

The second day of the Middle Fork "inside cattle herd" drive we went the rest of the way down Placer Gulch to the Middle Fork of the John Day River, made a right turn through the outskirts of Bates, a company logging town, then a left turn across a wooden bridge to the Middle Fork Road. We had to hold the cattle after crossing the bridge, because if the cattle behind saw those across the river going in the opposite direction, we had a real problem—they would try to turn around.

After we hit the road, we would go the ten miles down the river to our cow camp, where we would leave the cattle in the "cat shop" pasture to mother up. At the end of any drive such as this it is always necessary to hold the cattle in a group to wait for the cows to find their calves (mother up). Otherwise, they will start running back to where they last sucked, which may have been at the ranch. We had all sorts of "disasters" on these drives, mostly consisting of separating a calf or calves from their mothers. This is called "leppieing" the calf if you don't get them back together again. The calf either dies from lack of milk or grows up very puny. One can tell a well-run cow outfit by the number of leppe calves they have—the fewer the better the outfit.

I must say right here that to a cow man there is a whale of a difference between a "cattle ranch" and a "cow outfit," the latter usually much larger and needing real cowboys to operate. Tough guys that shoe their own horses, know how to handle a rope and who don't whimper when the going gets tough.

The next day after leaving all of the pairs at the cat shop pasture, we arrived bright and early back at cow camp to separate a certain number of pairs for each of the many "inside" pastures we had at the Middle Fork. This was probably the most fun day of the year for those of us who liked to "cowboy" because we put all of the cattle in the yard around the cow camp cabin and mothered up each calf with its mother—a certain number at a time, as stated, for distribution amongst the various inside pastures.

It is a real "science" to mother up the calf with the right mother. It has to be done right, or leppes are created—as I noted above, a major bugaboo on a cow ranch. The mothering-up process requires a good cutting horse to be fun and easy, or as one cowboy said, "to make fun out of hard work." I had the little mare, "Cojo Canella," which I bought off the Cojo Ranch in Santa Barbara County. She was "part cow" when it came to cutting. The horse has to sense which cow belongs to which calf and act accordingly. Then, when you have the two together, it has to move on them in such a way that they are taken out from the rest of the herd and moved through the gate through which you are cutting. Preferably, with a big crew, the whole process can be done in any corner, the pairs just cut away and the rest of the herd held in the corner. This makes the work go faster than cutting them through a gate, but requires a larger crew.

At the Middle Fork cow camp, we always cut through a gate.

One man with Dorro and I and perhaps some of our savvy kids made up a good crew. There are times in this process when a contrary cow will really make the horse and rider have to work, run fast, and pay attention or the job won't get done. I would usually take at least two cutting horses to ride, so as to not have to wear out one horse. This is a common failing I had—riding a good horse too hard. I would get so wrapped up in the work that I thought at the time that it was necessary.

With advancing years, perhaps, one is inclined to look back on such hard days and rides with a touch of arrogance or superior feeling which says, "It wasn't all that important."

Why, when we are young, do we insist on doing things the hard way in so many instances? The erudite sophisticated broker Harold Chase used to say merely, "Youth must err."—and perhaps that covers the subject.

As I look back on those hard riding days I have mixed emotions. In some respects it was necessary to push myself to the limit to get the work done, to pay the mortgage at the bank, which at the time I thought no one but me appreciated. But, with what meager wisdom that hindsight has created, I can also believe that I could have accomplished the same thing with a lot less effort, and easier on everyone else, if I had relaxed a little more and let myself and those around me, mostly the help and family members, have a little more fun in the process of getting the work done and the bills paid. My Type A personality showed.

**FDS on Buck at Strawberry Lake on Oxbow Ranch**

**("Buck" earned his name!)**

**FDS on snaffle bit colt, Oxbow buildings in background.**

**Oxbow Ranch house from east lawn**

**(note bridges across creek running under the house.)**

**FDS on Dusty at the Oxbow Ranch gate.**

**Note the brand symbol over the gate.**

Trailing Cattle—the "leads" coming home in the fall.

Vaccinating at the home corrals.

The horse is named "Cojo Canella," the best cutting horse FDS ever owned. (Foaled at Cojo Ranch in Santa Barbara, California, sister of "Cojo Rojo" which starred with Marlon Brando in the movie *Appaloosa*.

**Oxbow Ranch home, north lawn**

**Citabria at the ranch—"Cowboy Airplane"**

**Hay windrows on the Oxbow Ranch**

**Inspecting the hay field.**

**Citabria next to haystack with FDS**

"Mothering up" the calves on Placer Creek after trailing from the home ranch.

**Horse powered hay buck --"Mass" and "Nellie"**

**Homing Pigeons released Oxbow airport in race to Portland, OR
Strawberry Mountain in background**

**Dewitt House at cow camp on the Middle Fork of John Day River**

**L-R Foreman Del Raymond, Cow boss Phil Newton.**
**Unk. tiny cowboy—resting on the trail to cow camp**

## Chapter 16

# FIRST YEAR REALITY

The first year we had the Oxbow was a tough one for me. I didn't know where anything was, everything was new, and the foreman, Wes Clark, delighted in having me do things the hard way. We were together, Wes and I, from dawn to dark. Perhaps the most outstanding time of hard work, real work, that stands out is getting ready for irrigation that first year. The irrigation water came out of creeks, mostly from Strawberry Creek and tributaries. We would first divert the water from the creek by means of either a permanent head gate, which was the first-class way, or by means of gravel dams scooped up with a crawler tractor. In the spring when the creek would run high, this was exciting work in itself. The water would be as high as the floorboards of the tractor, and one always was concerned that it would rise up to cover the cooling fan so that it would "motorboat" right through the radiator. Then the electrical system might short out, leaving the tractor stranded with me on it in the middle of the raging torrent. Actually, the first year at the ranch,

Wes did all the cat work. This was looked upon as one of the major jobs – most important, because if the dams weren't put in right, the irrigation would not get done properly. After the water was out of the creek because of the head gate, or the cat-made dams, it would be transmitted through a series of ditches throughout the ranch. But to actually spread the water from these minor or major ditches, it was necessary to place manure dams at strategic spots.

We would haul manure with a tractor and wagon. But that first year, Wes had us pitching it on the wagons by hand. There were two hydraulic front end loaders that could have done this job mechanically, but he chose for us to do it by hand. Now, if I had any "smarts" about the routine at the time I would have picked up on this, but at the time I went along pretty much with anything he wanted to do because I felt it was imperative to have him that first full year show me how the ranch had been run all those years he had been on it—about 25 years, since his childhood. Well, this manure hauling by hand got into some hard work, about two weeks of it, and I know now he was just trying to wear me out, maybe for the fun of it. Or maybe he figured that I had so much money borrowed that I was going broke anyhow and he just wanted to hasten the process. Maybe he sought to bring back the former owners, under whom he had a free reign to run the ranch as he pleased.

It wasn't easy that first year, but I stayed with him—putting in the time, anyway. There was no way I could match him for brute strength. He was as strong as a bull. I mentioned before that, when shoeing a horse one day, he got perturbed by the beast, and picked him up physically and threw him to the ground. It proved to be too much for his back and he had ruptured a disk. He had a spinal fusion, and after coming from the operation with a cast on his back he went right to haying with the cast on. It had left his back in excellent shape, however, which I can attest to by the way he could pitch manure.

I, on the other hand, just managed to hang in there with him and get enough pitched on the wagon so as not to look too bad— depending on who was looking.

It took three to four weeks to get all the water turned on and spread. The idea was to put the entire ranch under water. In normal years we got the job done, but in the drier years the lower end of the ranch was always a little short.

After the water was turned on and the cattle trailed out thirty miles to the Middle Fork permit, and to the North Fork permit out thirty miles in the opposite direction, we had a little "breather"— about two weeks—before the fourth of July which by tradition was the start of the haying season. We started on July Fifth as we could always find a field that was ready by that time.

We had to start earlier than most ranches because we had more hay to put up, and we didn't get through until later than most. It irked me somewhat to hear another rancher brag about getting through haying before me, until I realized that he was only putting up 10% of the hay that we were. We hired high school and college boys to work on the hay crew and never had trouble finding them, they came to us. The word had gotten around about what a time we had at the Oxbow getting the hay put up. And that the haying lasted longer than on other ranches so they had a chance to make more money as well. I would get out my time book (which I still have) as the boys would start calling in June. Also in later years I phoned some myself that I knew were good workers, and put together a crew.

Wes told me that first year that the stacking job was critical. The work of the man who stayed on the stack to pitch the hay around to make a good stack that would shed water was critical. The stacker directed the front-end loader man driving the *Hydraloader* tractor as to where to place the loads of hay. If this wasn't done properly the stacks would not even stand up, let alone have a good top so they would shed moisture and not spoil.

We mowed the wild grass hay with power mowers attached to Ford Model 8N tractors, raked with Farmhand pin-wheel rakes, and then bunched the loose hay. For the bunching process we used draft horses pulling *horse bucks*. The horse buck was quite a piece of equipment for one such as me that was raised with draft horses. They are also known as "sweeps" in some parts of the world and are basically a rake that is pushed with horses. The rake teeth are made from lodge pole pines with the bark stripped off so the hay will slide on and off the teeth. The horse bucks went down the wind-rows sweeping the hay into bunches. Then the power bucks, one ton trucks with the rear ends turned around so that they ran backwards with the teeth forward of the drive wheels, would push the bunches into the stack yards where the *Hydraloader*, lifted the bunches on to the stack.

It was a great system, and fast.

The power bucks could push hay bunches at a high rate of speed—twenty or thirty mph—into the stack yards for stacking. The boys loved to run the power bucks, even though it was terribly dirty, dusty work. Only young people could take the punishment day in and day out. Of course, I ran one intermittently, as I did all of the equipment on the ranch.

The first day of haying was always a circus, teaching the boys how to run the equipment. When we started haying each year on the Oxbow Ranch it was like a Declaration of War in that our entire energies were directed and focused toward getting the hay "up." We kept the hay crew corralled at the bunk house which was attached to the main house. If their equipment needed fixing or just plain maintenance they would be there so that it could be done at night after supper. The rule was that all equipment had to be fixed in the evening so that it would be ready to go first thing in the morning.

Another little thing we had to do was to go back on standard or "slow" time for haying, because on daylight time the dew was still on the hay in the morning making it too wet to stack. We got used to it, but it was a bit odd to be on a different time than the rest of the community.

The other ranchers in the area did not have to go to standard time because they did not have the amount of hay to put up that we had. The plain and simple fact was we ran more cows than anyone else in Grant County so we had more work to do.

In 1961, the first year we had the ranch, just before haying was to start, a man showed up at the ranch looking for work. But he asked in a very uncommon way—specifically asking for the hardest job on the crew—that of hay stacker. His name was Walt Mackey and he was a miner. Actually he was more of a prospector because he was looking to strike it rich, not just make a bare living. Walt turned out to be the answer to our prayers as far as hay stacker is concerned because he really knew how to do it, making the best looking stacks in the country and enjoying the process. Where most men would have to come down from the stack to rest, Mackey stayed right on that stack until it was finished. Also, he was one of those people who always gave some comic relief when the going got tough. As hay stacker he drew the top wages on the crew—$12 per day rather than the $10 the others made, plus room and board.

Every year Walt said that was his last year to stack (it was the only work for wages he did all year long. The rest of the year he spent in the mountains prospecting and hunting.) But each year about a week before the Fourth of July, I made my annual pilgrimage to his cabin in the mountains to talk him into coming down to the valley to stack hay. He always came. The first few years it was by Model A Ford and when that gave out it was by a 1938 Ford ex-ambulance of which he was most proud. He called it his "little Lincoln." One year just before haying I got a phone call in the middle of the night from the John Day Jail, from Walt, drunk as a hoot owl and saying that he had been arrested for drunk driving in Prairie City. I told him to wait until morning and I would be down. I was there in the morning and sure enough there was Walt with both hands on the jail house bars, looking put-upon to say the least. I posted his bail and he spent a good portion of his summer paying me back the fine for his mistake.

Everything else on the ranch went to pot when we were haying. The cattle just had to get along without us because we could think of only one thing—getting the hay put up. The longer it went on the more frustrated we became. It was not a matter of *if* there would be any breakdowns on a given day, there always were, it was rather a matter of "what is going to break next?" I spent a good deal of my time chasing after parts for the equipment. Oddly enough there were no equipment dealers in the John Day Valley, the nearest being in Ontario, some one-hundred miles away, or in Baker, some eighty-five miles away. My little airplane made the parts acquisitions a lot easier and gave me some great relaxation away from the big problem—getting the hay put up.

When the day finally arrived when the last stack was up, usually sometime toward the end of August, it was cause for a great sigh of relief. In later years we threw a party for the crew, and that was a lot of fun. We usually had it right on the lawn at the ranch around the swimming pool.

## Chapter 17

# RUSTLER SURPRISE

A very interesting sequence of events occurred in the fall of the first year we had the ranch. Wes and I rode horseback every day gathering cattle on the Middle Fork. Of course, I had no idea how to go about gathering eight hundred cows and calves in the Middle Fork Valley and from the top of Vinegar Mountain to the top of Dooley Mountain—Vinegar being close to nine thousand feet and Dooley over six thousand feet. Generally, it was a matter of chasing the cattle into the valley and placing them in holding pastures until the bulk of them had been gathered. That first year I did not have the little airplane to spot cattle so it was a more lengthy process. Most of the gathering took place between the first of October and early November and the cattle had to be placed on the lush aftermath of the meadows for approximately ten days before shipping so the calves would have the opportunity to recover from the trail and put on some more weight.

At any rate, that first year Wes indicated that he could not understand why we were not gathering cattle more quickly, telling me that it was a lot slower than usual. We generally trucked our horses to the top of Dooley where we would jump them out of the truck and start to ride. Sometimes we trucked the horses all the way to cow camp ten miles down the Middle Fork River and ride out from cow camp.

On one particular day, though, for some reason we chose to ride from the base ranch instead of trucking. As we rode up the highway past Mel Kelly's place, Mel came out and offered to let us jump our horses into his truck and take us up to the top of the mountain. I thought this was exceedingly generous of him and we accepted.

I must digress a bit here so that you will get the full impact of what was about to transpire. After the purchase of the ranch had been completed, I became acquainted with Mel because the prior owners had taken several of the good saddle horses with them and we were in the market for a few. Since the Oxbow is a "horseback ranch" there was always a lot of riding to be done taking care of the cattle and we needed at least forty head of saddle horses.

Mel was a very personable fellow, cowboy all the way through. As a matter of fact, he was a pickup man at many of the largest rode-os in the west from the Cow Palace to Cheyenne. He was the fellow who rode up beside the bucking horses and pulled the cowboys from the broncs after the whistle blew. He was really good at it and had lots of friends as you can well imagine since he was essentially in the "rescuing" business, extracting cowboys from killer horses. His real profession, though, was trading horses and he always had quite a few for trading purposes. Sometimes he would go up into Canada and come back with truckloads of them for selling to ranchers in the John Day Valley and elsewhere. I probably purchased a dozen horses from him that first year. But in the fall after concluding one transaction, he made a strange statement.

He said, "You know, Don, I'm just a poor boy. I have to lie, cheat and steal in order to get along." This comment came right out of the blue and I thought it very strange, especially that word "steal."

Well, getting back to this cold fall day when Mel offered to truck our saddle horses to the top of Dooley Mountain—I got in the cab with him and Wes rode in the back of the truck with the horses which was not unusual. I believe Mel had a young boy with us in the cab, too, and that was why Wes had to ride in back. As we were going up the highway, Mel said, "Don, I went in the cattle business myself and we had a branding yesterday over at Ontario."

I thought this was an extremely strange remark because it was well known that Mel was always hard up and I could not figure out how he would have enough money to go in the cattle business. I soon found out when I got a call from a brand inspector to come over to Vail, Oregon, to inspect some cattle that might belong to me.

I went over to the Vail Auction Yards and looked at about thirty -five head of Oxbow cows that had the Oxbow brand obliterated by a Block A brand. Further, the brisket dewlaps on the cows which we used for a range mark had been cut off. But they were definitely our cows. On some of them you could see the tail of the Oxbow brand jutting out from beneath the Block A $\boxminus$, but there was no question that they had been re-branded since the brand inspector had followed some calves that were running at the sides of the cows through to slaughter and inspected the hide from the inside. They were definitely bearing Oxbow brands!

There were also some of the neighbors' cattle whose brands had been obliterated in the same manner and re-branded with the Block A. The Block A brand was registered to one of Mel's children. At any rate, the stolen cattle were traced to Mel Kelly. As I recall about one hundred fifty head, including about seventy head of ours were in the bunch—more stolen cattle by one individual than any individual in the history of the Oregon Brand Department at the time.

Mel was swiftly convicted and sentenced for cattle stealing. However, he was so popular, primarily due to his occupation as a pickup man at the rodeos, that a group got together to petition for early release. He was paroled from the Oregon State Penitentiary at Salem about six months after he was incarcerated and came back to live in his place in the John Day Valley in the house by the road to our summer range.

This incensed me to the point that when we were trailing about one thousand five hundred head, including calves, down the road by his place the following fall I did something a little out of character. I was riding a huge horse named "Tiny" who liked to jump. I jumped the fence into Mel's front yard, rode up to the big window of his living room and just sat there, staring at him. He came to the door eventually, out onto the small open porch and carefully passed the time of day with me.

I must confess I talked in rather menacing tones.

He moved away not long afterwards.

There is just something about a cow thief in cattle country that's not appreciated. I guess it's because it's hard enough to make ends meet and pay the mortgage at the bank solely from the calf crop without having a "silent partner" such as Mel Kelly.

From the outset the Oxbow experience was for me the ultimate. It was what I had dreamed of doing—owning and operating a real honest-to-goodness cow outfit. Everything we did was a challenge for me and I tried to do it right. Of course with all the borrowed money, usually about a million, which in the '60's was a lot more money—like ten million dollars—than it is today, it was imperative to survive financially for me to do an excellent job of running the outfit. The Production Credit Association in Portland from which I had the large operating loan was always looking over a borrower's shoulder, especially at loan renewal time in the fall when the results of the year's operations were analyzed and a determination was made regarding whether one could obtain another loan for the coming year. The ideal for the PCA was for the majority, if not all of the operating loan to be paid off each fall from that year's sale of cattle. (This only happened once for me, the last full year I operated in 1972 after Dorro and I were divorced and I'd married Helen—more on that later.)

Dorro and I went to Portland at renewal time. I took a hand-held computer with me and developed a budget the night before going to the PCA offices in the old Equitable Building to review the budget with the Assistant Manager, Len Mascal. It was really a good feeling to get his approval of the prior year's operations and to hear him say, "There should not be a problem when the loan committee considers your application at the next meeting."

He would never commit himself that the loan would be approved since he didn't have the authority to do so.

## Chapter 18

# BEGINNING OF THE END

One Sunday morning Dorro and I were feeding cattle in the Hagberry Barn. I believe that it was about 1966. By now we had been operating the ranch for approximately five years. Without any pre-warning I told Dorro that I had reached the momentous decision that working dawn 'til dark and then continuing in the office at night was not something that I cared to do for the balance of my life. In other words, in brief, we had to sell the ranch.

Selling a ranch as large as the Oxbow is not an easy task. Even though as Sherm Gutridge said, it was the "best ranch out of doors." At least in the 1960's there were not many people with enough financial resources to swing the deal, and that also wanted to take on all the problems that a large cattle ranch entails. It takes a very special kind of individual. We listed the place with various brokers and it was shown from time to time but many years passed before a buyer appeared.

Before we get to that, though, I want to say right here that problems developed between Dorro and I. We fought a lot, mostly over inconsequential things which seemed important at the time. Once, after such a ridiculous argument in retrospect, although it seemed important at the time, I took off for a little solo skiing at Bogus Basin north of Boise. After skiing awhile, I skied up to the lift at the bottom of the mountain and there was a beautiful young gal with a goat skin wine bag held high in the air, pouring the red nectar into her mouth. I couldn't resist stopping and striking up a conversation—and having a little wine. We skied together and she was really a great skier. Gayle was a student at Boise State, about twenty-two years old. We got along so famously that we decided we had to go skiing at a better place, Sun Valley. That very day, in mid-afternoon, I drove her to the house where she lived with her sister, who was married. Gayle packed up and away we went to Sun Valley!

What a trip!

Gayle was the best skier I had ever encountered to that date and loads of fun, a real outdoor girl. Our friendship continued for many years after Dorro and I had separated and I seriously considered marrying her, but "something" (another girl) intervened.

Arriving back at the ranch from skiing at Sun Valley with Gayle, I found Dorro gone from the ranch. I was advised she had taken a trip to Bend, one of our favorite destinations for skiing. I had a few beers late in the afternoon and then decided that since she had reportedly just left, I would jump in the little Citabria (N833OV) airplane and spot her on the highway. Just exactly what I would do after spotting her did not occur to me, but it seemed like a good idea at the time. Therefore, I went across the road to our little airstrip, fired up the Citabria and took off.

It was getting dark.

At about this time, I realized that perhaps flying after "a few beers" was not a good idea because I seemed to be not "all together." By this time it was really getting dark, so I made a 180 degree turn back to the ranch and landed without incident. Whereupon, I jumped in the Oldsmobile (a few beers never bothered driving like they did flying) and took off for Bend to find Dorro. Arriving about mid-night at one of the motels we usually stayed at when skiing, I saw her little Blazer parked in front of a motel room. Checking the Blazer out first, I noticed that there were two cocktail glasses in the cup holders.

This gave me strong suspicions as to whether she was alone in that motel room!

Not knowing exactly what to do, I did the obvious and knocked on the door!

Dorro's voice cried out "Who's there?"

There were muffled sounds of movement within but no one answered the door.

I really wanted to get inside that room so I did it the cowboy way—I took a few steps back from the big window, ducked my head upon which was my usual large Stetson, and crashed through the window amidst flying glass!

The first thing I saw was Dorro at the back of the motel room looking into the small bathroom, looking upward I might add with a very concerned expression on her face!

Whereupon I rushed to the bathroom door and immediately noticed the screen from a little window pulled away. Of course, I then confronted Dorro about who had been with her in the room.

No answer was received other than "No one."

After further discussion, we went to bed and made love.

I definitely detected that this was not the first time for Dorro that particular evening. But I must confess right here that it was quite hypocritical of me to be chasing after Dorro and a paramour when I had just returned from Sun Valley and spending a couple of nights with Gayle.

We are all "sinners" aren't we?

I must have made a quiet entrance into the motel room in spite of the crashing glass because we were not disturbed further that evening. The next morning I went to the office and made arrangements to pay for the glass and also made arrangements with Dorro to meet her at the lawyer's office we had been using for ranch business.

Upon arrival at the attorney's office, we discussed a divorce. I appreciated the attorney for his ethics, because he tried to dissuade us from divorcing and actually convinced us to go into counseling. We did go into counseling in Portland with a gentleman counselor considerably older than us by perhaps twenty years. After three sessions of baring our souls separately to him, he counseled me to "divorce her and the sooner the better!"

I didn't think counselors were supposed to do that!

By this time, the ski season was in full swing. My trusty employees at the ranch had everything under control. It was a quiet time of year before calving started. As I recall, it was right after Thanksgiving. All that was going on was feeding of the cattle and routine checking to make sure there were no big health problems with the herd. Also, it was a continual job to keep the machinery repaired. However, it was a quiet time of year and I decided to take the advice of the marriage counselor and get a divorce. Packing up a few things I drove to Boise because I had decided that an Idaho divorce was better than Oregon divorce because the residency requirements in Idaho were quite lenient and as I recall the grounds which I had, adultery, based on the Bend incident and Dorro's later confession of the name of her paramour (whom I had contacted) would play better in Idaho than in Oregon.

I rented an apartment in Boise and stocked it with bare provisions, with the intent of establishing residency on advice of counsel. Come Christmas time, 1970, I could not resist the urge to go home for Christmas, which I did. We had a family Christmas together in the traditional way, but the day after Christmas I returned to Boise to continue the Idaho residency requirement without telling Dorro that I was leaving. Rather than remain in the apartment in Boise, however, I leased a condominium in Sun Valley from my Idaho attorney. It seemed like a better place to have fun, which it certainly was. Soon after arrival there ensued an evening at a satellite operation of the Sun Valley Lodge named "Trail Creek Cabin." The snow was deep, bob sleds were in operation, sleigh bells were ringing and the mood was festive. As I entered the bar, I noted a very, *very* attractive blond at the bar, wearing a beautiful mink coat. Whereupon I joined her there, introduced myself, and we had a few martinis together and dinner.

Susan was an excellent conversationalist, turning out to be the "grass" widow of Dean Martin's musical director. She was a dress designer of some note with her own shop in Studio City, California, right next to Hollywood. After dinner, we retired to my condominium to get better acquainted, which we did, but without consummating anything. Primarily I can assure you, due to her resistance. However, I did receive some encouragement by way of an invitation to contact her for dinner the next evening after skiing. We didn't arrange to ski together because obviously she was a beginner and I wanted to hit the "black diamond" trails. Sure enough, however, the next evening we had dinner and there ensued the beginning of a beautiful friendship—and promises to meet again.

At about this point for some reason I don't remember, I decided that reconciliation with Dorro was advisable so I discontinued the Idaho residency and went back to the ranch to pay attention to business with the start of the calving season.

The reconciliation was of short duration.

It actually ended when we were in Portland on business and Dorro insisted on remaining in the City without me to attend a ground school for pilots of some kind. The problem for me was that also staying at the hotel where the seminar was to be held was a guy named Tex in whom I suspected Dorro to be interested. We had a big argument about this which ended in Dorro jamming a crutch— which she was carrying due to a horseback accident— into my mouth.

I left town without her.

There was also another incident involving Tex and Dorro.

At one point, when we were deep into our disagreements, I learned that Dorro had gone to John Day at a time when I knew Tex was also there. I drove my pickup from the ranch and scouted the streets of John Day, concentrating on the motels.

I was expecting the worst.

Sure enough, there was Dorro's Blazer parked at a motel next to the rig I knew Tex was driving. I inquired at the desk of the motel regarding the room Tex had been assigned, walked up to the door and knocked.

(It had no big window through which I could crash as I had done in Bend!)

This time, Tex opened the door and there was Dorro seated in the back of the room, as cool as a cucumber. They were just "talking about things" she said.

Right.

I departed, letting them continue their "discussion" without further incident.

There was also one other relationship Dorro had that must be mentioned because it figured so prominently in my state of mind. There was a fellow named Charlie at the Flightcraft Beechcraft Operation in Portland with whom we had socialized from time to time. However, one day Dorro informed me that she had also visited Charlie, who was very much married, at his little ranch near Bend. This got to me quite a bit because at this point I was not trusting Dorro.

Of course, at the same time, I was being most hypocritical because she had no reason to trust me either!

At any rate, this particular relationship between Dorro and Charlie came into real focus when I was at the Physician's Hospital in Portland recovering from a minor operation and Dorro was to pick me up on a given day at about 1:00 p.m. When she hadn't shown up by 4:00 pm I had the bright idea of checking at the Prineville Airport to see if our airplane had landed there. The reason I chose Prineville to inquire was that Charlie had acquired a ranch near there and perhaps even had a house in the locality. Sure enough, the airport operator told me that our airplane was parked there. So when Dorro arrived at the hospital at about 6:00 pm I delicately inquired where she had been—delicately only at first. She made up some story about getting away from the ranch as soon as she could and had not stopped any place along the way! There ensued a confrontation about her stopping in Prineville.

The conversation was not pretty.

The foregoing incidents emphasize the "War of the Roses" type relationship Dorro and I had. In retrospect, I accept *more* than fifty percent of the blame. However, it must be said that I was not, in my opinion, the sole cause of our divorce. Blame should be shared.

## *Divorce Arrives*

After the crutch incident, Dorro and I wound up making a mutual decision for her to visit an attorney in Portland named Wendel Gray: purpose, divorce. Gray had an associate named Nathan Heath. He actually did most of the work involved with representing Dorro. Nathan and I got along fine. We negotiated a Marital Settlement Agreement that included me receiving the Oxbow Ranch and the debt thereon and awarding Dorro an approximate half million dollar compensating payment represented by my promissory note and a second mortgage on the ranch.

Other minor things included Dorro receiving the Twin Bonanza which she requested, the Tahoe cabin at Marla Bay which we had purchased from her father, all of the household furniture, furnishings and equipment which she desired which were extensive since the Oxbow house was ten thousand square feet with fifteen bedrooms and ten baths including a large one in the bunk house attached to the Main residence.

The date was set for the hearing in St. Helens, Oregon, a suburb of Portland.

I flew to Van Nuys for a rendezvous with Susan before the hearing.

A day or two prior to the date set for the hearing, I received a phone call in the evening from Wendel Gray. He told me that Dorro wished to reverse the whole process and reconcile. I received that phone call in Susan's bedroom and was definitely in no frame of mind to reconcile at that time—although later that changed too.

I flew back to St. Helens for the hearing with a few loose ends in the MSA to resolve. Dorro and I were completely at odds, unable to communicate on any subject. I later learned how strange it is when two people who have been in love, deeply in love, reach an impasse to the extent that the communication lines are completely closed. Nothing either of us said was received by the other in any reasonable way.

Ah! Sweet mystery of life.

After the divorce was finalized, we were officially not husband and wife, although it didn't seem possible. We went back to the ranch where I was needed to continue running the operation and Dorro had no place else to go. We therefore resided in the big old ranch house at opposite ends of the place.

But we could not avoid continuing the feud.

It was obvious that Dorro must move as I needed to be there to run the ranch. She had always enjoyed the Bend area and located a small 250 acre ranch next to Sisters, Oregon. She made a deal for it, requesting my assistance in her arranging for credit to consummate the deal. It seemed odd sitting in the bank vouching for Dorro's credibility in what seemed to be a quite small transaction at the time, $50,000.00 down on a $250,000.00 deal for 250 acres on the edge of Sisters which would appreciate in value in the ensuing years to be worth, I'm told, millions.

At least I can look back on this and say that with the money Dorro received in the divorce she was able to make this transaction. She made the deal. She's entitled to reap the benefits which I am sure she did and has already shared with our four children.

## Chapter 19

# HOLLYWOOD

After our divorce, I delivered the Twin Bonanza to Dorro and started looking for a smaller airplane for cross-country travel. I had the little Citabria at the ranch, but that was strictly for observation purposes, spotting cattle, checking fence lines and irrigation. I located a Beechcraft Baron which had two hundred sixty horsepower engines in Eugene and bought it for $30,000. It was a fun airplane and it soon learned its own way between the Oxbow in Eastern Oregon and Van Nuys Airport, next to Studio City where Susan resided and had her dress shop. I wore a fairly deep groove in the sky between the Oxbow and Van Nuys flying down, as I recall, about twice a month. What fun it was!

I was forty-six and in excellent health and my girlfriend was thirty-two and likewise healthy. We partied, big time.

She had two small children, ages approximately eight and ten, who were lots of fun. As far as my children were concerned, Eva was in school at the University of Colorado, Doug in college at

Corvalis, Christine also in college in Colorado and Mary living with her mother and attending High School in Redmond.

I flew Susie and her children up to the ranch in the fall during gathering time. I fixed Susie up with a small horse named Andy to help bring the cattle from the Middle Fork back to the base ranch. Coming back down the highway from "tip top" pasture (the top of Dooley Mountain), Andy took a notion to "take the bit in his teeth" and sort of ran away with Susie. She became extremely irate and from that point on I began to reserve judgment on how long I wanted to be around Susie.

After 23 years with Dorro I had an aversion to strong willed women and it looked like I was becoming involved with another!

## Chapter 20

# THE END OF AN ERA

### *Uncle Otto and the Rosemere Herd*

Aunt Eva and Uncle Otto were in Maquoketa during the winter of 1969 attending to their business at Rosemere Farm when Otto fell ill and was receiving in-patient treatment for his medical problems at the Maquoketa hospital when he suffered a massive heart attack and passed away.

When I got the news I immediately made arrangements to attend the funeral in Maquoketa. Many cattlemen attended the services. It was a large affair at which several cattlemen and I spoke regarding our respect for Otto.

Aunt Eva was devastated but carried on with her life as well as she could. I was made the executor of the Will, which left all his property to Aunt Eva. After the services and other business, I flew back to California with her and arranged with a close friend and neighbor, Carolyn Peterson, to attend to her needs.

The big question in Otto's estate was what to do with the Rosemere Herd. I finally decided that the best possible answer was to bring the pure-bred Angus herd to the Oxbow and operate it for the benefit of the estate.

It was quite a thrill to me when these super high class cattle were unloaded at the ranch. They had withstood the truck ride from Maquoketa in great shape and my heart swelled with pride at the sight of these great cattle grazing in the special meadows that I assigned to them.

I had to obtain the services of a skilled herdsman to work with the Rosemere Herd and found him in the person of Clint Hudson. Clint was an old hand with purebred Angus cattle and was then employed with an Angus herd located near Lompoc, California.

Flying into the airport near his location, I actually talked with Clint in the cabin of the airplane and convinced him that it would be a great opportunity for him to work on the Oxbow with the great Rosemere Herd.

Otto Battles had established the herd in 1898 with the gift of twelve females from his mother, Laura Battles.

I guess the most significant thing I did with the Rosemere Herd while I had it was to purchase a very special bull calf at auction with the idea of using him as a herd sire. I flew to the auction which was held on the grounds of the MonReposa Ranch near Jerome, Idaho. Since I'd divorced Dorro, I was accompanied on the flight by my girlfriend, Suzy and my herdsman, Clint Hudson.

The calf's name was Chapparal, and he later became Supreme Champion of the Angus Futurity stock show held at Reno in 1973. Actually my purchase was of a half interest in the bull calf with Bob Thomas of Baker, Oregon. After I had sold the Oxbow I retained ownership of my half interest in Chaparral. Later, while on the round-the-world trip with Helen (you'll meet her later) I received a cable from Bob in Bangkok, Thailand, offering $30,000 for my ½ interest.

I accepted.

Since I had only paid about $2000 for the half interest, the calf was a pretty good investment!

There's nothing like going to Bangkok and successfully marketing an Angus bull located in Oregon!

Ah, serendipity!

## *Aunt Eva*

During this period of 1971 and my commitment to Susan, Aunt Eva, had been living in Santa Ynez since Otto's death. She was becoming unable to care for herself. She was firing the twenty-four hour nurses that were necessary for her care about as fast as Carolyn Peterson (a neighbor who had also served as Uncle Otto's secretary) and I could hire them.

I enlisted Susie's assistance in traveling to Santa Ynez, getting Aunt Eva in the airplane and flying her up to Prairie City with the idea of placing her in the nursing home there. This was kind of an underhanded operation on my part because I owed Aunt Eva so much for having raised me, becoming my surrogate mother so to speak.

At first, Aunt Eva, Susie and I stayed at the ranch while the operations were continuing with the cattle in a normal fashion. Susie would stay with Aunt Eva and some friends she had brought along during the day while I was working on the ranch.

I remember at the conclusion of one day Aunt Eva drew me aside, bless her heart, and said in effect with respect to Susie, "Watch your step, be careful."

I took this remark to mean that Aunt Eva didn't think she was quite up to our standards.

That remark probably put the death knell on Susie.

By the time I flew Susie and her friends back to Van Nuys, we were fighting like cats and dogs.

## *Helen*

The next course of events in this saga concerns the receptionist at an internist's office in Portland, Dr. Richard Kosterlitz, whom I had seen for a routine medical checkup. This receptionist caught my eye, you might say, when I first visited the office. Not only was she extremely attractive to me, but her dad was a well-known cattleman in Eastern Oregon who was the then President of the Oregon Cattlemen's Association.

After I had returned to the ranch following the big fight with Susan, I remembered Helen and phoned her one night. (I had seen fit to obtain her phone number previously). I made a date to meet her the next evening at the hotel at which I planned to stay. I flew to Portland for our first date, met her at the hotel, entered the bar with her together and proceeded to immediately fall in love over martinis.

She was such a fun person!

What a sense of humor!

We had a lot in common, having both been raised in the cattle business, albeit, she on a commercial cattle ranch and me on a purebred operation.

As I recall, this first date was along in November of 1971. By the second date, I suggested we become "steadies." She said she had another commitment, but that could be taken care of and the deal was sealed. We were going steady.

The next move was my purchase of an engagement ring before Christmas that year.

Things moved swiftly.

Me, in my small plebeian mind, figured not only was this the gal for me, but we should do it before December 31ˢᵗ so we could file taxes jointly!

Helen, being a business woman, understood perfectly. She had never been married before, which was another factor appealing to me since that meant she came with no "baggage." The date was set between Christmas and New Years to take place at Helen's folks' residence at Vail, Oregon, near the location of their extensive ranching, farming and cattle feeding operations.

## *Misgivings*

There was an incident on Christmas Eve 1971 that must be mentioned. As I often look back on it, it was a watershed event.

I placed a call to Dorro from Vail, Oregon, where we were visiting Helen's brother and sister-in-law in their ranch home. I told Dorro I was having misgivings about marrying Helen. I suggested to Dorro that we get together the very next day at the ranch with our kids who were visiting her. She advised she had other plans although she did say it sounded like a good idea. I've often thought that if that decision of hers not to meet me was otherwise, life would have been completely different for me. Although I can say that looking back upon it, I would not change anything because my life thereafter afforded many experiences and rewards that I would never have had if Dorro and I had reconciled.

## *Misgivings Dropped—"I Do" Helen*

The wedding took place on December 29, 1970 at Helen's folks' residence. It was quite a large affair for a home wedding with lots of cattlemen. After the ceremony we drove to Boise and caught an airline flight for Hawaii where we had a delightful honeymoon for about one week, maybe two.

We then returned to the ranch to go to work as calving was beginning. Helen took another look at that big 10,000 square foot house and, being an interior decorator as well as a doctor's receptionist, she made decorating plans of which I approved wholeheartedly.

It takes a lot of carpet to do a 10,000 square foot abode and that is what she bought, all at her wholesale prices. She also bought lots of furniture which we needed because Dorro took everything except a plaster cast of Mary's hand sitting on the mantle over the fireplace. She left me a note, "I thought you might like this, but if not I would be happy to have it returned."

Right.

The house blossomed as it never had before. It was cleaned up from stem to stern, everything but the bunk house which remained in a rather "utilitarian" condition. Helen and I continued to operate that ranch and in 1972 for the first time in 12 years, the ranch showed a profit! The PCA was paid off.

We were sitting pretty but I was oh so tired of running the crew and making ends meet. In addition, after about a half a day in the saddle my legs were going numb and I frankly did not know how long my body would continue to take the abuse of being the No. 1 Cowboy on a large cow outfit.

Cowboying is just hazardous work if you are in it to the extent that I was. It's exciting, of course, but it is a proven fact that one can tire of excitement! (It leads to exhaustion). I had never quite agreed before with that concept, but at the time my body was telling me it would be better to sell out at a profit and get into some other line of endeavor—maybe even another cow outfit with a different set of problems.

I had learned how to operate the ranch intuitively to the extent that I could tell by the way a man was approaching me what had gone wrong—and believe me, things always went wrong. It's the nature of life on a large cattle ranch that is being operated on a practical basis just to be able to pay the interest on the debt at the bank!

The place continued to be listed on the market with various Realtors. Occasionally it would be shown, but no acceptable offers were made. However, along in the latter part of 1972, I received what appeared to be a legitimate offer of $1.5 million from a wealthy East Coast publisher named Scudder. It was accompanied by a $100,000 check which was delivered into escrow pending the title report. The escrow holder, Grant County Land Title Company, deposited the check in its account. About two weeks passed, the title report was issued, and I received notification from Mr. Scudder that he didn't like the state of the title. I was curious because I knew there were mining claims on the Middle Fork deeded land that were not to his liking, but I did not feel that the escrow instructions were such that he had a legitimate excuse for not proceeding with the deal. I called the title company and expressed my misgivings and the officer told me that the $100,000 check had not cleared and that payment had been stopped after having been deposited in the Title Company's bank. As an attorney myself, I didn't see how this could have been done—until I checked with the bank upon which the check had been drawn and found that Mr. Scudder was on its Board of Directors. I assume that he had means through this connection to reach into the Federal Reserve clearing system and stop the payment. I thought about suing the man. Things were going so well at the ranch that I decided not to sue, and also to remove the ranch from the market.

About three months passed and I again returned to my earlier concern that my body was telling me that it couldn't take the abuse I was giving it much longer. The long days in the saddle, the numb legs, and the rest of it wore away at me. So I re-listed the property, not at the former asking price of $1.5 million, but at a new price of $2.5 million.

Scarcely 30 days passed after the listing when the Realtor showed up with a fellow that wanted to look at the place. This was early in the morning about the time I usually lined up the work for the crew which took place out at the horse barn, giving each man his instructions for the day. I told the Realtor that I didn't have time to talk to him right then but that if he could wait for about an hour or so I'd be available. I then proceeded about my business and in about an hour I was introduced to the prospect by the Realtor who introduced the gentleman as Dan Lufkin who had just flown in his Lear jet to Redmond, the closest large airport. As soon as I heard the words "Lear jet" I thought, *this may be for real.*

I gave Mr. Lufkin my full attention.

The Realtor was dismissed, so to speak, because Lufkin wanted to talk directly with me. This was about 9:00 AM and I showed Dan around the place at the base ranch. Then we got in the little two place Citabria airplane to view things from the air including a trip up to the Middle Fork cow camp which was about thirty air miles away where we had made a landing strip. It was a short strip, perhaps twelve-hundred feet long, and the elevation was close to six-thousand feet so there weren't many airplanes that could land successfully—or take off. As a matter of fact, there was no airplane of which I am aware that ever landed at that strip other than me.

After showing Dan around the cow camp pastures we returned to the plane. During take-off from the short strip Dan said, "Don, couldn't you have made this a little bit shorter?"

I will hand it to Dan who was used to flying in Falcons or Lear jets that he didn't hesitate to fly with me in the little airplane. We flew back to the ranch and discussed a deal in the ranch office. Dan said he liked what he had seen and would like to buy it. We didn't have time for a written deal but based on our conversations and a hand shake, he delivered to me a $100,000 earnest money check at the full asking price of $2.5 million.

With the escrow started and the title report going again, Dan sent his CPA out from the East Coast to go over the ranch books and to examine the ranch in detail, including riding horseback with me through the pastures. The accountant carried a tape recorder, which was unusual in those days, and recorded everything I told him. I remember at one point in response to one "dude" question, I said, "Dan will just have to find out about that himself."

This tickled the accountant who made appropriate remarks into his tape recorder. After that, Dan came out to have another look around before the deal closed. I put him on a horse named Pepper because Pepper was noted for his easy riding gait and his intelligence and safety. I warned Dan that it was the spring of the year and we had the irrigation turned on. Bog holes could appear suddenly without warning so I instructed him not to ride far from me because I knew where all the bog holes were.

We set off at an easy lope across the pasture known as the "Front Olp" and had only gone perhaps a half a mile when Pepper put all four feet in a bog hole and down they went with Dan going off in the mud! We managed to extract Pepper from the bog hole and Dan got out as well, a little the worse for wear.

I was embarrassed but it didn't kill the deal.

The deal was closed before the 5th of July, our traditional day for the start of the hay season. Nobody works in cow country on the 4th of July. We considered it the American way for everybody to get drunk on that particular day, not only in celebration of our Independence Day but prior to the beginning of our "war" on the huge hay crop which the Oxbow always produced.

When I sold the Oxbow to Dan Lufkin that July day in 1973, the sale included the Rosemere Herd. Tom Hudson continued to be the herdsman until Dan sold the herd at auction at the ranch a couple of years after he had bought the ranch.

Dan's primary interest was in cutting horses and he built the largest indoor roping arena in Oregon, at the time on one of the meadows near the ranch house.

*Chapter 21*

# THE LAWSUIT

After the deal was made with Dan Lufkin, arrangements had to be made through escrow to pay off the $500,000 Note that I had given Dorro as part of the divorce settlement. Of course, the settlement was made on the basis of the ranch being worth what we had paid for it plus the cattle and machinery—in other words at "book value."

The sale to Lufkin at around $2.5 million was a substantial gain over the original $1 million, none of which belonged to Dorro. I recall taking the papers needed in escrow to clear the encumbrance over for her to sign. When I told her how much the sale was for she became livid.

Such a tirade.

She pushed me out of her house on the little ranch at Sisters.

The reaction was no surprise to me.

I knew how angry she could become. However, I was not prepared for the service upon me a few days later of a Summons and

Complaint with the Plaintiffs being my daughters, Eva and Christine and Dorro as Guardian Ad Litem of our then minor child, Mary.

I could scarcely believe my eyes as I read the Complaint. It stated that for several years Dooley had been mailing to me the sum of approximately $400.00 per month "for the children's education" and accused me of converting these funds to my own use. The Complaint had been prepared by a Prineville attorney, Jim Bodie.

Well, to have my own children suing me was a blow like I had never had before and it was a completely unfair accusation. In point of fact, what had happened was those $400.00 checks were deposited in the only bank account we had. Most of the checks were payable to both Dorro and I and we deposited them in our one bank account which we used for both ranch expenses and living expenses. The accountant segregated the personal and business expenses so the tax returns would be accurate. As far as the children's education was concerned, three of them were in college and we paid their college expenses out of that one account. Obviously, the law suit was a sham and frivolous to the extreme. Dorro had benefitted from that $400.00 per month as much as I had. So had the children, since they received anything they needed from us for their education.

Only Douglas, who at the time was 21, would have nothing to do with suing his dad. Eva and Christine were completely under the control of Dorro and Mary, who was in High School, didn't understand what was going on. I remember being so distraught over the unfairness and just plain shock at having my own children suing me for money I didn't owe them that I went into a spare bedroom at the ranch, bawling like a baby. I suppose this was the only time I have ever come close to a nervous breakdown. I couldn't stop hyperventilating. I had to do something about this horrible fix Dorro had caused for me—*Hell hath no fury as a woman scorned.*

Our daughter Eva was 25 and married to a Texas rancher, Jacko Garret, whose ranch was near Alvin, Texas. I figured that she was old enough to know better so I bought an airline ticket to Houston to talk to her. Renting a car, I drove to the hospital where she was employed as a physical therapist. I could not find her and a receptionist told me that she had word that I was coming and when I came in the front door of the hospital she went out the back door.

This may be wrong, but that was my information. I didn't even get to see her because as soon as I learned she appeared purposefully avoiding me I said, "To hell with it!" and flew back to Oregon without seeing her. I guess I'd just awakened to the reality that this was not an earth-shattering event—this law suit.

The total amount sent to us by Dooley was about $25,000 and that is what the law suit requested. At the time it was not a large sum to me. Rather than go to Court and argue with my two daughters and Dorro or even explain the truth about how the money had been utilized, I decided the best thing to do was just to pay what they wanted. I hesitate to use the word *they* because I'm sure Dorro was behind the whole thing.

Douglas was not a party to the law suit, but I paid him the same amount as the girls received from the litigation—even a bit more. I can look back on these events now with dispassionate hindsight and see it for exactly what it was. Dorro was so upset over me profiting from the sale of the ranch that she had to seek retribution.

Dorro never recovered from my profiting from the sale of the ranch. I believe it was this event and not the divorce that caused her to treat me not as a second-class citizen, but more like a ninth or tenth class citizen. Down through the years she has ridiculed and criticized me at every opportunity with some minor exceptions. It's too bad that she had to become bitter. Had she been bitter over our divorce that would be one thing, but becoming bitter because I profited from the sale of the ranch seems rather petty.

As a result of the bitterness and contempt which Dorro has held for me, my attempts through the years to get together with her and our four children for annual family meetings—or at least once every few years—have been unsuccessful. I have never criticized Dorro to any of our four children. I don't know what she has told them about me, but maybe this story will set the record straight—at least from my point of view.

Her point of view is no doubt completely different!

After the divorce I did have some sessions with a therapist in Studio City suggested by Suzie. Her name was Maxine Durr and she listened to my entire tale of woe. In the final analysis, after explaining the many years of turmoil that had been occurring with Dorro, Maxine shook her pretty head and said, "Well, she never loved you anyhow."

I believe that says it all and relates back to what she had told me after we were engaged, "I will marry you so long as you understood that I don't love you!"

How sad.

However, better days were ahead and they still are!

# Chapter 22

# THE AEROSTAR

Allow me to digress a bit.

In 1972, not too long after Helen and I were married, I decided I had to have the world's fastest reciprocating light twin airplane, an Aerostar 601. It was designed and built by Ted Smith who was then residing in Van Nuys where his factory was located. Ted had started the Aerostar program with the American Cement Company as a backer in 1968. They built a lot of airplanes before the American Cement Company decided it didn't want to be in business with Ted anymore and withdrew, selling the program to Butler Aviation of Texas. At the time I became interested in the airplane, Ted had repurchased the program from Butler and was more or less hand-building the airplanes in Van Nuys at his hanger, looking for a partner to go back into mass production. I found this particular airplane at a dealer in the San Francisco Bay Area and traded him my little Beech Baron for a 601 Turbocharged Aerostar. It was the seventh one manufactured with turbo charged engines.

This *bird* was a *going machine* capable of three-hundred miles per hour at its certificated ceiling of thirty-thousand feet. Not being pressurized, however, it was necessary to wear oxygen masks—a real nuisance. At any rate, during the deal making phase of the sale of the ranch to Dan Lufkin I picked him up in the Aerostar at the Hillsboro Airport at Portland and flew him back to the ranch. I was really proud of the Aerostar until I looked over at Dan as we were climbing out of Portland on the North side of Mt. Hood and said to myself, *What are you thinking, Don? This guy is used to flying in a Falcon jet.*

After concluding the ranch sale prior to July 4, 1973 with Dan Lufkin—that's Lufkin of the Wall Street firm Donaldson Lufkin Jenrette—Helen and I loaded all of the delicate things in the Aerostar. Then we loaded some minimal furnishings and personal effects in our Jeep station wagon with the mattress tied on the topside luggage rack and headed toward Friday Harbor in the San Juan Islands. She drove the Jeep and I, naturally, got the easy end of the stick by flying the Aerostar to the little airport at Friday Harbor.

One of the reasons we chose Friday Harbor for a retreat was that the author Ernest K. Gann lived there. It was not long after we settled into our rented water front house at Friday Harbor, next to the Ferry landing, that I became reacquainted with Ernie and his wife Dodie. Dodie Post was the ski instructor Dorro and I had at Squaw Valley in the Stanford days, a former women's Olympic skier and captain of the Women's Olympic ski team. Helen and I and Ernie and Dodie had several fun evenings together. I have always felt very privileged to have known Ernie Gann who is still regarded by many as America's foremost aviation author with such classics as *The High and the Mighty, Fate is the Hunter* and *Band of Brothers.*

His own favorite, though, of all of his work was *Song of the Siren*, a tale of Ernie and Dodie's solo trip around the world in a small sail boat. You see, Ernie was an avid sailor as well as a pilot, and just coincidentally, a great guy.

# Chapter 23

# AROUND THE WORLD IN 80 DAYS

Helen liked to travel.

While I was chairman of the Santa Maria Airport Commission I met an airport designer named Leigh Fisher. He and his wife later visited us at the Oxbow. At some point we decided we should take a trip around the world together. At the time Leigh was working on airport design for the Island of Guam in the Western Pacific. Meeting them in Hawaii, we booked passage on Air Micronesia through the Western Pacific, including stops at Guam, Saipan, Yap and Palau.

At Palau we tried chewing some of the betelnut leaves that the natives use as a mild narcotic. We were snorkeling off a small island, engaged in viewing the coral reefs in the vicinity, when a rain squall came up. It started raining hard. I looked behind me and there was Helen crying out with the classic outstretched arm going down for what appeared to be the third time. As rapidly possible, and I'm not much of a swimmer, I reached her and in spite of her struggles managed to haul her ashore.

I feel certain that if I had not done this she would have drowned. She was grateful and I praised the Lord that I had been able to save her.

After Palau, we flew to Kuala Lumpur. We rented a car and drove to Singapore, then flew to Jakarta and drove through the Island of Java.

What a trip!

It was like a time machine going back several centuries with the vehicular traffic being mostly carts pulled by water buffalo. The fields were tilled by natives in the rice paddies with hand rakes.

After Jog Jakarta it was over to Bali, the Island of 10,000 temples, for more adventure. We then flew to New Delhi at about which point Leigh and I had words about some insignificant matter and they changed their plans to continue the trip with us.

This was indeed unfortunate but these things do happen.

Helen and I continued to Thailand, India and New Zealand. We were then approved on the North Island at Wellington by the Government as being qualified bidders at the sale of a beautiful station that was to be auctioned at one of the wool auction houses. I didn't have quite enough wherewithal to make the purchase, but I often wonder where my life would be if we had made it. These crossroads occur in everyone's life and as the ball player, Yogi Berra said, "When you reach a fork in the road, take it."

We ended our journey with a short stay in Paris before returning via Seattle to Friday Harbor. I must add that in Thailand, I purchased a fine piece of jewelry for each of my three daughters, but forgot to declare them on the General Declaration when arriving at Seattle. Of course, a Customs Officer saw the jewelry in plain sight in my luggage and I had to pay a hefty fine for my feeble alleged attempted "smuggling."

**FDS taking possession of his new Hughs 500C helicopter**

# Chapter 24

# HELICOPTERS

Being relieved of the daunting task of running the Oxbow Ranch at a profit to pay the interest on the money borrowed at the bank, it did not take me long to find some other engaging activity such as learning about helicopters. It was during a trip to Van Nuys for maintenance on the Aerostar at Ted Smith's hanger (he was the only one that knew how to fix them at that time) that I noticed a Hiller helicopter sitting by the hanger. I went over and examined it and arranged for a lesson from the owner—and I was hooked. Back at Friday Harbor, not having anything else to occupy my attention, I arranged for flight lessons and helicopter flying with Eddie Lamotta at Boeing Field.

Eddie was an old-time helicopter guy whose brother Wes Lamotta had founded Columbia Helicopters. As the first outfit to engage in heli-logging, Wes developed a technique of "flying the load" which was unique at the time. It was a matter of the pilot look-ing down and by very minute movements of the controls always hovering over the load, whatever might be on the end of the line, so that the load could be landed exactly—and I do mean exactly, where it was supposed to go. Eddie was a character. He had several very young Veteran Vietnam helicopter pilots working for him as instructors and they were the best. I soon learned how to hover, was soloed, and then started to have lots of fun!

I tooled around the Boeing Field area which was close to the Longacres Race Track. I tended to fly in isolated spots doing practice maneuvers required for the flight exam. Eddie himself gave me the flight exam for a commercial helicopter rating.

I passed.

Whereupon I immediately started to talk to people at Hughes Aircraft about purchasing a little reciprocating engine helicopter designated at that time as a 300C. It was a variation on the Model 269 helicopters that I had been flying in training. I hopped an airliner down to Los Angeles and was checked out at Long Beach Airport in my new 300C by the Hughes Aircraft pilots. It is a much more stable machine than the 269 so it didn't take long, perhaps an hour or two at the Long Beach Airport to be checked out.

Helen and I each had a small bag as luggage but the problem was there was no luggage space other than baskets on the outside of the helicopter on each side. We tied our bags in the baskets with clothes line rope, got in the little machine, lifted off and headed for Friday Harbor. What a fun trip! We ran into a little weather in Northern California and had to do a low level cross country-type maneuver through the Siskiyou Mountains. Small helicopters don't have much range so it was necessary to stop every couple of hours for fuel. The top speed of the little machine was about 100 mph. We did make it, however, and flew across the Strait of Juan de Fuca to Friday Harbor.

## *Got a Bigger Bird*

Scarcely two weeks went by before the Hughes Aircraft helicopter salesman, Woody McClinden, contacted me and told me that I really ought to take a demonstration in a 500C Turbine Helicopter. I met him at Phoenix for this purpose and one ride in the Turbine helicopter convinced me.

The 300C cost me $55,000 and he allowed the trade in about a month after it had been purchased at the full purchase price. The well-equipped Hughes 500C cost $150,000.

I went to Culver City to the Hughes Aircraft Factory facility to learn how to fly turbine helicopters. My instructor was Bob Faires. Having set a non-stop record for helicopters between Los Angeles and Florida in a 500C, Bob enjoyed considerable helicopter fame. He taught me how to autorotate from behind the deadman's curve at 200 feet AGL. Quite a trick! It required a very delicate touch. We landed on a heliport atop the Occidental Building in Hollywood which at the time had a fine restaurant directly below the heliport. What class!

After I was certified as a turbine helicopter pilot, the first passenger was, of course, brave Helen, and of course our destination had to be that heliport atop the Occidental Building for lunch! We then departed in grand style for Friday Harbor. When I say "grand style," I mean as compared to the 300C, since the 500C had a back seat and plenty of room for luggage inside the aircraft. Not only that, but it was well equipped with state of the art navigational systems for helicopters. We could literally land any place we wanted to—by a restaurant or a motel or a mountain lake.

What fun it is to be "mobile in space" with the ability to stop, back up, or go sideways in the air — the next thing to feathers!

Not long after acquiring the 500C, I contacted our friend Ernie Gann and told him he had to go flying with me in my new chopper. I was granted permission to land next to his studio where he had written such classics as *Fate is the Hunter*. His studio was a converted chicken house. But the chickens were still there on his ranch a short distance away and I scared them on landing.

We flew around the San Juan Islands and I tried to convince Ernie that he should write about the courage of helicopter pilots flying behind the deadman's curve all day long when transporting sling loads of logs. If that engine quit at such low level, unless they were able to duplicate Bob Faires' technique of auto rotation from a high hover, they were dead.

Ernie didn't think much of the idea.

He said he didn't understand helicopters and didn't want to understand helicopters.

This is a shame in my opinion because no one could write adventure stories involving courage like Ernest K. Gann.

One of the fun things that Helen and I did with that helicopter (Identification 711DH, special numbers for Don and Helen) was to start at the Canadian line and fly all the way to Mexico at low levels over the beach at perhaps 100 to 200 feet all the way.

Then coming back toward Friday Harbor, we made it a point to land on every tall building that had a heliport at the time on the West Coast. There was a very neat helipad on a parking garage in Portland, for instance, and one in Seattle also. At the time we needed no clearances to land. We just determined where the heliports were and landed without any problems. It was always fun to land downtown Portland on the top of a parking garage and take the elevator down to street level.

## *Real Estate from the Air*

At about this time I decided that I needed a business purpose for the Hughes 500 so I studied up and took the Real Estate Exam in Oregon and became a ranch realtor. I figured that there was no way to look at a ranch like from a helicopter. We obtained a duplex apartment in Klamath Falls and I signed up as a real estate ranch salesman with a broker in Klamath Falls. The duplex was cool because it had a garden which was large enough for me to land the helicopter. I also obtained hanger space in a large hanger at the Klamath Falls Airport. From time to time, I would fly out and show ranches especially in Eastern Oregon. This lasted for a few months, the culmination of which was to find another ranch for myself.

## *Another Ranch?*

The Bob Lister Ranch out of Paulina, a 1,200 cow outfit, was for sale and I decided to buy it. I worked with the owner, Phyllis Lister, the daughter of Bob Lister who had died, and a deal was made through her attorney— none other than Nathan Heath, Dorro's divorce lawyer!

All of the details of the transaction were almost finalized, even the cattle had been counted. But I decided it would not be a good idea to go ahead with the purchase of the Lister Ranch so I made up some legitimate excuse to get out of the deal and flew the helicopter down to Santa Monica for the necessary training to get my Airline Transport Rating (ATP).

I made the trip without Helen, because we had decided to divorce. In spite of the planned divorce, though, I phoned Helen and she came to Santa Monica.

I finished the flight training with her present and obtained my

Airline Transport Pilot Rating. We returned to Klamath Falls together even though our divorce plans had been finalized. There was a brief hiatus in the divorce proceedings, however.

The first time we flew to St. Helens, at the same Courthouse that Dorro and I had obtained our divorce, we took Nathan Heath and his wife with us in the helicopter making it a sort of bizarre festive occasion. Helen and I got along so well that at the Courthouse we decided we did not need a divorce and got a continuance to work things out.

It was kind of an unusual event because I was able to land the helicopter right adjacent to the Courthouse in a parking lot.

However, the reconciliation didn't last long and the divorce was finalized with Nathan Heath, Dorro's attorney, also representing Helen. In the final stages, Helen and I sat in his office and worked out a property settlement agreement in a few minutes. For our 2 ½ years of marriage, I made her a "compensatory" payment of $200,000 cash. Helen's brother told her that he thought this was pretty good pay for her!

She was well worth it.

# Chapter 25

# THE NAPA VALLEY YEARS

### *From Cows to Grapes*

Not long after the divorce from Helen in 1975 I was returning
from a trip to the Bay Area in the helicopter. I looked down and
saw a glider port next to Calistoga in the Napa Valley. Not having
anything better to do, I made a 180 degree turn and landed. I entered
glider pilot training, starting another phase of my flight experience.

Not only that, I started looking at the vines, the grape vines in
the beautiful Napa Valley. I told Helen about them. We talked to
Realtors especially one named Bill Bonsell. He had a beautiful vineyard listed for sale that could turn a profit he said.

We looked at it.

It was eighty acres, with seventy-five acres of vines and had an
appealing owner's home. Not only that, the owner Bill Griffin, a
real gentleman and good business man who had been operating the

vineyard as such, showed a profit and loss statement that was very attractive. He was asking $1 million for the vineyard.

A key ingredient in any vineyard operation if you don't have your own winery is to have a "home for the grapes." In this particular instance, the home for the grapes for Mr. Griffin was Bealieu Vineyard, owned by Heubline, Inc. They had contracted to take all of the production each year. Without a grape contract, a grower is at a big disadvantage because grapes are very perishable and there is no time to negotiate a sale of the grapes after they are mature and ready to pick. It has to be done in advance.

In accordance with the tradition, any given winery will usually contract with the grape grower for several years' future production, thereby assuring the grape grower that he will have a "home for the grapes" and the vintner will have the product.

During the negotiations for the Griffin Vineyard, Bealieu served notice on Mr. Griffin that they were canceling the contract, which they had the right to do under the terms of the contract. Thus, I with no knowledge at that time of how the grape business worked, other than what Bonsell was telling me, felt that the deal was no longer viable. However, Lee Knowles, the President of Bealieu Winery with whom I was talking at the time about the cancellation of the contract, made a remark, a chance remark, "Well, even without our contract it is worth something."

This prompted me to take a chance and offer Mr. Griffin to continue the purchase at a $250,000 discount, with $750,000 being my new offer.

He accepted.

In order to make it a family operation, I loaned my son, Douglas, $250,000 and Helen took a third at $250,000. I had the other third.

### *"Sokol Vineyards" was born*

We had a great "crush" in the fall of 1975, picking up about $200,000 for the crop. The vineyard was debt free so I figured we could find a market for next year's grapes someplace and hopefully another contract. Doug moved to a small house in Oakville near the vineyard and became a stalwart partner in the operation. He is a quick learner and soon mastered the vineyard operation under the guidance of Rusty Hall, the long term foreman and former owner of the property. When he owned it the place was planted to vegetables.

Rusty had a terrible injury while he had owned the property. He went into a burning barn to rescue a tractor, was caught in the fire and suffered horrible burns. His head was terribly scarred, with no hair, and hands burnt so badly they resembled claws rather than hands. But he managed to continue his farm work, doing it in a very high class manner. He was a great guy, one whom I will always remember as being one of the outstanding individuals I have known. I admire someone who rises above injuries such as these and continues their life in spite of the odds which destroy lesser people.

Helen and I became acquainted with most of the grape growers and vintners in the Napa Valley in short order. The social life was great and the wine greater. However, Helen and I continued to have problems. Of course, we were not married any longer, but we nevertheless felt committed—up to a point. That point was exceeded after a disagreement when Helen said "So long," loaded up the Jeep Wagoneer that we had had at the Oxbow and drove away. "It is with a heavy heart," she said in a goodbye note I found on my desk.

She drove over to Sacramento where she stayed with her aunt for many months thereafter and from time to time I would visit.

I admire Helen and appreciate all the good times we had together.

## *Days—and Nights—of Wine and Roses*

After Helen left, Doug and I continued to operate the vineyard. I remained in the social whirl and was introduced to the daughter of a prominent grape grower, who at the time owned more acreage in the Napa Valley than anyone else.

Her name was Dawne. I genuinely, honestly, fell in love.

She was about 40 and had two great sons and a great father who was also a cattle rancher with a large cattle ranch near Alturas. We attended my daughter Christine's wedding near Bend at which Dorro's father, Dooley, was also in attendance. We fought after she danced, I thought a little too closely, with another fellow in attendance. Our relationship contained many quarrels, all of them over more or less meaningless items as is so often the case. On one trip to Mexico in my new Bellanca airplane, I remember that we felt like bitter enemies by the time we had returned.

On one trip to Portland, I had purchased an engagement ring for Dawne. She took one look at it and said, "Let me go back and look at some other rings." I thought the one that I had picked out was nice but it was a very good jewelry store and there were a lot nicer ones. She brought back a nicer one, about three times the price of the one that I had picked out.

I bought it for her. In a little while, she gave it back to me.

Then we reconciled and I gave it back to her. I never saw it again and didn't ask for it back!

There were many other fun girlfriends besides Dawne, none of which led to serious relationships. I can't even remember their names! Having a beautiful vineyard that almost operated itself, with trusted employee Rusty and partner Doug, living alone and with two airplanes at my disposal, seemed to attract the opposite sex.

## *Helipad*

Soon after Helen and I had purchased the vineyards, I told Doug that when I first looked at the vineyard I was fascinated with the flat roof on the garage. I just knew that I had to have a heliport. Doug, being very handy at construction, built me a helipad on that roof after beefing up the underpinnings. It was a little tight to land on but it worked.

Thereafter, I used the helicopter not only for personal transportation but also to dry the grapes in the fall of the year. I blew the dew away from the vines early in the morning so that the pickers could start picking earlier. The grapes could not be picked while the dew was still on the vines because too much of the dew wound up in the grape gondolas and diluted the sugar content so the wineries insisted that we wait to pick until the grapes were dry.

By using the helicopter we were able to pick sooner, thereby affecting quite a major improvement in the harvesting routine. I dried grapes with the helicopter for other growers as well. However this was not enough work to make the helicopter economically viable, so eventually I flew it to Tucson with Helen where I thought it could be more readily sold. It was. It was a fun machine and I will always look back on that helicopter ownership period as being a happier period by reason of having the helicopter with which to work or play.

**Debra's graduation from Pacific Union College, Angwin, California as a Registered Nurse**

# Chapter 26

# SWEET DEBRA

One fine day in 1976, I landed my airplane at the Angwin Airport where it was hangered on a ridge high above the Napa Valley.

I stopped at the vegetarian restaurant in Angwin for a late lunch, probably about 2:00 PM. As I entered the restaurant, I noticed a young gal with flaming red hair seated at a table all alone. Angwin being a Seventh Day Adventist community with Pacific Union College adjacent, it was a vegetarian restaurant. Always willing to take a chance and be humiliated, I stopped at the table of this young lady and said, "May I join you?"

Of course, she was at the only occupied table in the little cafeteria at that time, but that did not seem to be an impediment. She appeared a little embarrassed, but said, "Okay."

We proceeded to get acquainted.

I bragged a lot.

I told her I'd like to have a date.

She gave me her number.

I then went on about my business. Perhaps three weeks later I got a phone call from Debra. She said, "When are we going to have that date?"

What a break!

We set a time and a place.

I took her to dinner in the evening at the Oakville Grocery Restaurant, about a half mile from my vineyard.

I was impressed.

I have to admit that one of the things that impressed me was her age. We were twenty-eight years apart in age. Miss Debra Anne Klingbeil was twenty-four at the time and me, fifty-two.

I must confess I am struck with younger women.

Our age difference didn't seem to bother. We dated. I took her to South Lake Tahoe for a show. Since we had the same room, I figured this is it!

It wasn't.

She held out.

I bought her a painting at the Hotel. She smiled. We flew back to Angwin. We had some more dates. Finally I told her this heavy petting is great, but I can't stand it any longer. She capitulated.

It wasn't easy.

We fell in love.

I was proud to be with her.

She invited me to fly her back to Marietta, Georgia to meet her parents. I did. I was impressed. I met her grandmother who said, "I approve and the sooner you're married, the better!"

On the way back to California from Georgia, flying the plane on auto pilot, Debbie and I started one kiss soon after departure—"a kiss to build a dream on"—and believe it or not that kiss continued until Texas perhaps four hours later!

Hard to believe?

Truth is stranger than fiction.

We dated more, flying up and down the West Coast as the spirit moved us. While coming back from the cabin I had inherited from my Aunt Eva on the Naches River on the east side of Mount Ranier, Debbie looked at me and said, "Let's get married."

I was flattered that such a wonderful young lady would have me!

So, I replied "Okay" and that was it—the best decision of my life and one that has stood the test of time.

In the meantime, I had been doubling efforts to find a buyer for the vineyards. I didn't particularly cotton to the wine grape growing business, maybe because I was more used to wearing Levi's and cowboy boots, not the bib overhauls and clod hopper farmer shoes that all the grape farmers wore. It just wasn't my style and I didn't have the capital or the desire to have my own winery.

In my view, I was therefore seen as a second-class citizen even though when they found out I was an attorney they elected me Chairman of the negotiating committee for the Napa Valley Grape Growers, selling grapes to Bealieu Winery.

The buyer for the vineyard finally did come along in 1978 in the form of a wealthy Iranian immigrant. I didn't want to sell it outright, I wanted to trade back into a cattle ranch, so we set up an escrow with a 1033 Tax free exchange in mind.

### Back to Cowboying—Nevada Style

I located a ranch in Diamond Valley, Nevada, about fifty miles south of Elko and flew Debra out to view the place before we were married—she fell in love with it.

It had a small adobe house and she told me she could fix it up

Debra and FDS's wedding at Marrietta,
GA home of Debra's parents—Dr. and Mrs. Robert Klingbiel.

"like a doll house," which she eventually did. The deal was closed and I bought a cattle ranch type pickup truck in Napa and drove to the ranch. Deb drove our Jeep Cherokee pulling a U-haul with more household goods as we migrated to the ranch in Diamond Valley.

We were very happy together, to say the least. I bought Debra cowboy boots. She learned how to ride (but not to rope). We were married on September 2nd. The vineyard deal was made just before the grape harvest season (the crush) began, and included a provision for me to keep the grape crop. I left Doug in charge of the harvesting and Deb and I went out in Nevada to gather the cattle off our new range with their fat calves to market.

Things had never been better.

I was selling both grapes and cattle that fall and it was the best straight income year I had before or since, about $500,000 ordinary income.

It was a lot of fun learning how ranching was done in Diamond Valley, Nevada. The weather and temperatures were not that much different than Eastern Oregon but the haying part was a lot different. The meadows on what we called the Broken Circle Ranch, because of the brand in that shape ⌒, were not nearly as productive as the Oxbow. The ranch had a large spring flowing twenty-five hundred gallons per minute year round of very high quality water at one hundred and one degrees. This hot spring was very impressive, as it must have been to Reinhold Sadler, the Governor of the State of Nevada around 1900 who homesteaded the place. As a matter of fact, the owner who sold it to the person I purchased the ranch from was a grandson of the Governor with the same name, Reinhold Sadler.

There was about one thousand head of very good desert-type cows on the ranch. But because of feed restrictions their calves did not weigh up as much as the Oxbow calves by any means. I figured the Oxbow cows on the average were producing close to four hundred pounds of beef a year whereas at the Sadler Ranch it would stretch things to say that the cows were producing three hundred pounds of beef per year. This, after all, is the real test for productivity of a cattle ranch—how many pounds of beef it will produce on average.

The buildings on the Broken Circle other than the huge metal shop were not nearly as adequate as those on the Oxbow. As a matter of fact, I soon decided that we would build a new horse barn and combination warehouse/calving barn. We put up metal buildings that were functional for these purposes but without anywhere near the "class" of the beautiful white trimmed in green redwood buildings that were on the Oxbow. It was definitely a second class outfit as compared to the Oxbow in most every respect (except the wife).

But then again, it only cost half as much.

Before the deal on the Broken Circle was concluded, I talked my daughter Christine and her husband, Randy, into coming down to the ranch and make a partnership deal, the same as I did with Doug on the vineyard. However, this deal was not consummated since it was not long after Christine and Randy arrived that they decided to divorce.

Christine stayed on as an employee but eventually left after a couple of years. We had a lot of fun with Christine, whom I love dearly, but I guess she just tired of the routine at the ranch. While she was there we built a roping arena. I bought about 25 head of Mexican roping steers and we had many evenings of fun practicing our roping skills. Christine always had good horses and she became a good roper. After Randy left, one of the neighbor's sons, Fred Bailey, came to work for us and he and Christine became bosom buddies. They made a great pair because they both loved to ride and rope and, incidentally, both chewed Copenhagen!

After Christine left, the ranch was not as much fun because we had to rely on hired help. The land and cattle market were rising and in 1981 I decided to sell the place at a substantial profit. It had cost about $1.1 million and I had a deal at $1.5 million. However, the down payment was non-existent and I had to pay money even though I was the seller to get the escrow closed. I had a Promissory Note secured by the ranch in the approximate amount of $1.5 million which brought in about $15,000 per month.

I thought I could get by on that so we moved to Santa Barbara, my old stomping grounds, and rented a large house on a quiet street near the mission. I toyed with the idea of going back to practicing law but didn't find any interesting opportunities. Our first son, Slade, was born in August of 1979 and we were having lots of fun with him although Debbie started working for one of the large department stores and Slade was put in day care a lot. He didn't like that. We were only in Santa Barbara a short while, however, when the cowboy life called us back to Elko where we purchased a house and about twenty acres near Lamoyle, east of Elko. The place had a barn as well as a house so we were able to bring a couple of our horses that had not been sold with the ranch. We improved the barn with a saddle room, had chickens and geese, and a garden.

It was pretty dull for me and I spent most of my time looking for another investment although I was severely handicapped with the large Promissory Note that no one seemed interested in exchanging for real property.

In September 1982, while we were still at Lamoyle, our second son, Taylor, was born.

I had another family started and it was great fun.

In 1982 before Taylor was born, Debbie and I had planned a trip with the Baptist Minister and his wife, Jim and Tori Wright, to tour Israel. In the last week or so before we were to depart, Debra decided that her pregnancy was causing too much sickness so I wound up going with Jim and Tori for a wonderful trip of about two weeks in Israel, traveling from the Southernmost to the Northernmost parts of the country. We rented a car and drove in the North through the Golan Heights and the headwaters of the Jordan to the South at the Dead Sea and Masada. I still have on my desk the New American Standard Bible that I carried with me. The Bible has been rebound because it was essentially worn out. A few years ago a visiting Catholic Priest graciously offered to have it rebound for me.

Debra was raised as a Seventh Day Adventist and I gradually converted. It was about ten years from about 1983 to 1993 that I was essentially a non-drinker of alcoholic beverages. As the cowboy song goes, "I don't have as much fun since I stopped drinking."

My thoughts on this are that I believe it is more fun when alcohol is consumed in moderation, easing the pain that life always carries with it.

**FDS and African ladies at the tomb of Joseph of Aramethia, Jerusalem, Israel**

**Christine mounted on damn good horse (as usual)**

## Chapter 27

# TROUBLE ON BROKEN CIRCLE

It came as no great surprise one day in 1983 when I received a phone call from our ranch buyer's law office that the buyer was on the verge of bankruptcy and wished to return the ranch to us. No surprise because he had been late on his monthly payments in recent months. I was actually relieved and glad to get the ranch back because I had missed the problems of ranch ownership. I accepted the return of the ranch and voluntarily cancelled the Note. I was shocked, however, at the dilapidated, run down condition of the place, machinery broke down and all of the cattle sold. This was in June, just about the time haying operations should begin. I got busy and repaired the machinery and started haying, but the crop was not nearly as much as we had produced before because the irrigation had been done improperly. I started looking for cattle to restock and wound up purchasing about a thousand cows in Idaho.

They were good Idaho cows but they didn't take to the Nevada vegetation very well. It has been my experience that it is very difficult to replace cattle on a large cattle ranch. Native cattle that are raised on the ranch are much better producers because they are fully acclimatized and basically know where to travel to get the best nourishment and to produce the most pounds of beef. We had a lot of trouble, consequently, with the Idaho cows. Debbie loves to tell of turning them out in the spring on the range and then having them come running back to the home ranch because they didn't want to rustle their own feed.

The ranch was not nearly as profitable after we got it back and had to use the Idaho cows for production. It wasn't easy but I finally managed to get it resold in 1985 for cash, but at a substantial loss compared to the first sale because in the interim both land and cattle values had declined for two years.

I did have enough cash left however, about $300,000, to finance my next venture.

# Chapter 28

# THE BUSINESS OF FLYING

Imade up my mind that rather than continue ranching on a reduced scale, I must try the flying business, namely a "fixed base operation." This is the industry term for an operator at an airport who engages in fuel sales, maintenance, instruction and aircraft rental.

I finally found one that looked feasible at Warrenton, Oregon, next to Astoria. The business was called the Astoria Flight Service, Inc., and specialized in maintenance, fueling, aircraft rental, instruction and charters. There were several aircraft included in the purchase including a Cessna 172, a Piper Warrior, a Cessna 210 Centurian, and a Piper Aztec Twin and a pressurized Beechcraft Baron, both on lease.

I promptly pitched in and did the necessary training to secure a flight instructor's certificate. I had two pilots who also instructed and flew charters. We had a maintenance department with one IA (Inspection Authorization) mechanic. We fueled aircraft and had an aircraft fueling contract for the military. It was a very small operation but one that was "hands on" as far as I was concerned and fun to operate.

I didn't know whether I could make a living at it, however, and soon discovered that there just was not enough business at the Warrenton Airport to produce a livelihood. I had purchased a house in Warrenton, a nice house on about 3 acres of land adjacent to a small stream. It was quite scenic but very damp since this area is noted for heavy rainfall, perhaps an average of sixty to seventy inches per year. After about three years it was apparent that the business was not viable so I took the only alternative I considered I had.

I returned to the practice of law.

## *Return to the Jealous Mistress*

My father always told me that "the law is a jealous mistress." He meant that it was time consuming to the exclusion of most other activities in which one might engage. I have found this to be true to a certain extent although operating a large cattle ranch is also time consuming as is being on call twenty-four hour, seven days a week in a flight charter business.

After completing the review courses at Stanford Law School, I seriously considered where we should relocate and finally decided that I didn't like the idea of returning to city life. Remembering buying cattle for the Oxbow out of Alturas in Modoc County, I decided to start there to investigate whether there were opportunities. Then I continued my search southbound in the rural areas of Northern California.

I drove to Alturas and soon discovered that things were dead there after talking to the leading attorney, Mr. John Baker. He was one of about five practicing there. That took about one hour.

## *Susanville, California*

I then proceeded south to Susanville where a firm, Kellison & Cady had been advertising for another attorney. I talked to Frank Cady first and then Craig Kellison, both of whom seemed impressed. It took about an hour for them to hire me to work for them with the view toward becoming a partner.

The pay was minimal for the time, $2,000 a month. But I felt that I could quickly become worth a lot more than that to them and work into a partnership. It was really weird after all the cowboying and playing I had done to start over again at the age of sixty-four.

Debbie stayed in Warrenton and I commuted about twice a month in the little Maule airplane that we had bought with the ranch and had used in the flight business at Warrenton. I had the little airplane equipped for IFR (instrument flight rules) and utilized this capability frequently between Susanville and Astoria.

The law business at Kellison & Cady consisted of a general practice and I was quickly assigned the criminal part of it. I also handled family law which neither Frank nor Craig were interested in. I had early successes in the criminal cases that came along and survived with the family law cases as well.

In 1990, the firm was offered the defense of Douglas Cecerle, charged with the first degree murder of his wife.

The case was assigned to me.

Although I had been trying cases before juries in the Justice Court, this was the first jury trial for me in the Superior Court. Neither Frank nor Craig were much interested in assisting, although I did discuss tactics and they helped me in defending Mr. Cecerle.

Early on at one of my first interviews with Doug at the county jail, he told me that he had no alternative other than to kill his wife which I thought very strange at the time because Doug was not a stupid fellow. I then learned that some six weeks prior to the incident he had consulted with a doctor of osteopathy in Chester regarding the depression he had been having which he assigned to a rather bitter divorce that he was going through. The doctor was, of course, sympathetic and over the phone, without even seeing Douglas, prescribed a six month supply of Prozac to help and hopefully bring him out of the depression. Instead of doing that, Doug found himself becoming very agitated, hypertensive and aggressive. After about six weeks on the drug, he received in the mail an adverse decision from the divorce court judge making what he considered to be an unfairly high assignment of income and assets to his wife. He became so incensed that he went immediately to the Y Market in the village of Westwood where he lived and purchased two bottles of Colt 45 Malt Liquor which he proceeded to chug-a-lug in a total of about 5 minutes. He then announced to the store keeper that he was going to his wife's home and kill her. This alarmed the store keeper enough so that she immediately phoned the Sheriff's Office in an attempt to get a deputy to follow Doug to his home perhaps half a mile away.

The deputy didn't get there in time, however.

Doug arrived at the house, the door was locked.

He broke a window in the door to gain access to the house and entered the room where his wife was sitting talking on the telephone. The telephone was an ordinary phone with a hand-held receiver which he wrested from her and proceeded to beat her on the head until she was unconscious.

Unfortunately, the two small Cecerle children observed this activity from a stairway.

At or about this time, the deputy arrived and placed Doug under arrest.

After being told Doug was taking Prozac, I did some investigation and found that there was a "Prozac survivor's" group in California and other similar groups elsewhere which had been formed to protest the legitimacy of the drug. They too had suffered bizarre ideation of violence just as Douglas had but luckily in most cases someone or something had intervened to stop them. What struck me most in these interviews was that in more than one instance, the person who had suffered such ideation had said, "I had no alternative" to doing what they had done—the exact words Doug had used.

I became convinced that the Fluoxetine Hydrochloride (Prozac) coupled with the alcohol consumed in a very short space of time had placed Doug on "autopilot" so that he didn't know what he was doing at the time he did the deed.

An Assistant Attorney General prosecuted the case, which soon attracted nation-wide attention. Television cameras were set up for the first time in Lassen County history in the Courtroom. All of this was quite a change for me from my cowboy and flying activities.

All I can say is I survived and convinced the Judge to rule that for the first time in the United States there was a causal connection between Prozac and homicide. The case made front page of the Wall Street Journal and Newsweek Magazine. After the trial Doug and I appeared on Primetime Live. Doug was not acquitted but was found guilty of second degree murder and sentenced to twenty-five years to life. He died in prison after serving several years of his sentence.

I did my very best for Doug and I believe the second degree murder conviction was not out of line with the deed committed although if the jury had believed that he was indeed "unconscious" because of the Prozac and alcohol they could have found him not guilty.

I had some very experienced testimony from a renowned psychiatrist, Dr. Martin Blinder, and a psychologist, Dr. Paul Berg, also from the Bay Area, who often worked with Dr. Blinder. (Dr. Blinder was the promulgator of the so-called "Twinkie Defense" in the trial of Dan White who shot San Francisco Mayor Mosconi and Supervisor Harvey Milk.)

I soon found that the practice of law in the 1990's consisted of how many balls one could keep in the air at the same time, because in the general practice of law in a small town one is inclined toward getting a lot of small cases most of which consume a lot of time. A lawyer is obliged to carry a heavy case load in order to make ends meet because no one case produces that much income.

After about four years with Kellison & Cady we came to a parting of the ways. For the years I'd worked for them I received as remuneration for my efforts 45% of the gross income that I produced. Actually, now that I've had the experience since 1993 of operating my own office, it wasn't such a bad deal.

# Chapter 29

# ALASKA

In the summer of 1992 when our son Slade was fourteen, we decided to fly our P Model V-Tail Bonanza to Alaska and tour the state. We took with us a tiny puppy that we named Amelia because of her flying adventures with us.

We covered Anchorage, The Kenai Peninsula, Fairbanks and points in between. We had a great trip as did Amelia who in restaurants would be nestled underneath Slade's shirt. She never let out a peep so no one usually knew that we had a dog with us with some major exceptions. We returned via Dawson City and the Northwest Territory and the Alcan Highway, more or less.

In 1995, I repeated the Alaska trip in the Bonanza with second son Taylor at the time almost fourteen. We went to a lot of the same places that Slade and I had gone but really wanted to get up to Point Barrow on the Arctic Ocean north of Fairbanks which we were unable to do because of weather. We found a lot of weather on the way back from Fairbanks.

Generally, when the weather got bad, Taylor would go to sleep.

About 2 years later, Taylor and I returned to Alaska and this time we made it all the way to Point Barrow arriving late in the afternoon on July 4th. We had to pay $55.00 extra to get the Eskimo refueling truck to come out to fuel us since July 4th is a celebration day for the Eskimos at Point Barrow. They were having Eskimo athletic competitions on the beach and the polar ice cap was visible a few feet off shore. Shortly after we arrived at the beach, we noted a foot race competition for men over seventy years of age and I was sorely tempted to compete. I felt this was my real chance for fame. Taylor was standing in front of me in shorts. Most everyone else were wearing parkas. He was obviously concerned about all the foreign looking activity. He told me that he would be embarrassed if I ran that foot race so I didn't do it and have regretted that to this day.

## Chapter 30

# HOME TO SUSANVILLE

After I left Kellison & Cady in 1992, I rented an upstairs office from Mr. Gary Woolverton, a well-known Susanville attorney. The address was 235 South Lassen Street, right across from the Courthouse. It was a great location and my law business prospered.

The most memorable case I had during the year I practiced from this office was for an old time cattleman named John Casey who was accused by a wealthy neighbor, R.C. Roberts, of branding calves owned by Mr. Roberts. Actually what happened was that the two herds would mix together because of poor fences, so from time to time they had to be separated. By this time in his life, John Casey was not cowboying but was relying on hired help. R.C. Roberts had always relied on hired help. Neither crews were very good so they were unable to properly identify calves as belonging to their respective owners and consequently they were branding each other's calves. Primarily, however, it was John Casey branding R.C.

Robert's calves for which he was prosecuted and hired me as his lawyer.

I felt right at home with this because of all my experience running the Oxbow and the Broken Circle where the neighbor's calves were either mixed with ours or were running together. Obviously they needed separating before any branding occurred and this entails "mothering up" small calves with their mothers and is somewhat of a "scientific" endeavor.

Inevitably mistakes are made.

Unfortunately, John Casey's reputation was not the best. As a matter of fact, he was a legend in his own time for living on the edge of the law, rightly or wrongly. Under the constraints of all of the legalities involved and the problem with John Casey's reputation, the jury came back with a guilty verdict. It was appealed and confirmed at the District Court of Appeal level.

In 1993 I was able to acquire an office building of my own at 110 South Lassen where I practiced for the next fourteen years. I continued with about a fifty percent mix of family law cases, farm and ranch law, criminal law, probate and a general business practice, sometimes referred to as "transactional."

I had a series of secretaries until 1998 when I acquired the services of Julie Johnston. That solved the secretary problem. Through perseverance and hard work, the revenue from the practice gradually increased so that by 2005 the gross exceeded $450,000.

Not bad for a small town practice.

### *Campaign for Judge*

In 1998 a local attorney named Ridgely L. Lazard was appointed Superior Court Judge. He replaced Joseph B. Harvey who had been

Judge since about 1977 until he resigned.

The Lassen County Superior Court has two Judges, so that when one retires while his term is still running, the Governor of California appoints a successor as the law requires.

At the time, Mr. Frank Cady for whom I had worked was also vying for the open Judge position. I definitely favored Ridgely Lazard over Frank Cady and wrote at least two letters to the Governor's Appointment Secretary favoring Lazard who was ultimately appointed.

Most of my law practice continued in Department 1 with Judge Stephen D. Bradbury who handled family law, unlimited civil cases, probate and criminal felonies. Department 2 was primarily criminal and felony law and motion and misdemeanor trials.

I had no trouble with Judge Lazard for a few years.

That changed when he became embroiled in a controversy with the Public Defender, Toni Healey.

Toni felt that he was biased and prejudiced against her and other defense attorneys and was unable to be impartial. Ultimately she specifically charged him under California Code of Civil Procedure Section 170.1 that he was biased and prejudiced and unable to be impartial in the *Turner* case. An outside Judge, Mr. Gaylan Hathaway from Mendocino County, was assigned by the Judicial Council to try the 170.1 and 170.3 Motion. Hathaway found that Judge Lazard was indeed biased and prejudiced against three Public Defenders, Toni Healey, John Dirk, and Rhea Giannotti and further, that he was unable to be impartial.

About this time I began inquiring when Judge Lazard's term of office would expire and was informed that it would happen in 2006. The idea of becoming a Judge was appealing to me. Previously I had been appointed Administrative Law Judge to hear Kahea cases at the

High Desert State Prison and found the wearing of the black robe a fine experience. Trying to do the right thing rather than having to advocate for one side or the other and trying to discover the truth seemed a step above being down "in the well"—having to zealously argue in favor of a client who sometimes was not all that appreciative of your efforts.

In 2005, as a further reason for my dissatisfaction with Judge Lazard, I became involved in a probate case, the *Lemons* case.

The father had died leaving an estate in Lassen and Plumas Counties. One of the beneficiaries, Greg Lemons, phoned me from Missouri and said that he had been appointed in the Will as Executor but that his brother, Jeff Lemons of Chester, had petitioned for Letters Testamentary. Greg instructed me to file a counter Petition to have the court appoint him rather than his brother Jeff. Since Greg was appointed first in the Will of his father, it seemed like a simple thing, which it was, to get him appointed rather than Jeff.

After a series of sales in the Estate, all of the money was sent back to Greg in Missouri under a Decree of Distribution to distribute the Estate between Greg, Jeff and Lori, a sister. I finally was able to get an accounting of the Estate from Greg and obtained a Decree of Distribution from the Lassen County Court instructing Greg to distribute the property, one-third to him, one-third to his brother Jeff and one-third to Lori. Despite repeated requests to follow the Decree of Distribution, Greg did nothing. We then learned that he had taken the Estate's money and purchased a farm in Missouri in his own name and in the name of his wife. In other words, he had taken the cash sent to him from sales of the Estate property and purchased a farm for himself and his wife. This was verified by the mother.

After securing the removal of Greg as Executor and becoming the attorney for his brother, Jeff , I enlisted the aid of the Lassen

County District Attorney to extradite Greg from Missouri with charges of theft and embezzlement. Greg was extradited and a Preliminary Hearing was held in the Lassen County Superior Court, Department 2, before Judge Lazard.

I testified to the facts at the hearing.

Lazard took a recess.

In a few minutes he returned to Court and announced his decision that there was no probable cause to hold Greg to answer for his crime because his brother, Jeff, the new Executor, had not requested the property be distributed!

This completely ignored the fact that the Court had previously ordered Greg to distribute the property. Further, at the hearing at my request the Deputy District Attorney had offered to reopen the testimony and present evidence that Jeff had, indeed, sent a Registered letter to Greg requesting distribution. Judge Lazard refused the request to reopen and discharged Mr. Gregory Lemons from custody, enabling him to return to Missouri to the farm that he had purchased with Estate funds.

I shook my head in disbelief at this ruling.

Knowing that Judge Lazard's term of office was up in 2006, I talked about this situation with local attorneys and in particular Toni Healey. Healy had been awarded the prestigious *Clay Award* for having disqualified Judge Lazard from hearing criminal cases because of his ruling in the *Turner* case. I offered to contribute and to work for a campaign for her to run for Superior Court Judge against Lazard.

She declined.

Another local attorney, Mark Nareau, decided that he would run, but in a few months changed his mind.

Then I got a call from Toni Healey, Lassen County Public

Defender, as the deadline for filing nominations approached in February of 2006. She stated on the phone, "Don, you have to run."

That did it!

I filed nomination papers in February of 2006 after much soul searching with Debra, Slade and Taylor, as well as other people. Another deciding factor was that, at a cocktail party a couple of months prior to my decision, I met a relative newcomer to Lassen County, Dr. Tom Gauthier, whose father was Chief of Police in Santa Barbara when I was practicing law there in the 1950's. When I told Tom that I was considering a run, he immediately stated he would like to help.

After I made my decision, I contacted Tom and he agreed to be my campaign manager. Tom had spent his career with a multinational corporation beginning in sales and rising to International Human Resources Director—picking up his MBA and Doctorate in Psychology along the way. He had never run a political campaign before but he was a world-class salesman and he told me, "Don, you're just another package."

Tom proved to be an invaluable ally as he and our friend, Rod Chambers, who owns the Sierra Broadcasting Company along with his partner, George Carl, became my campaign "committee of two."

Prior to filing the nomination papers, I discussed my candidacy with various people—including a trip to the Chambers of Judge Ridgely Lazard. When I told him I was going to run for his seat he asked me, "What don't you like about my judging?"

Rather than get into a discussion on this subject, I just said, "It (being a Judge) is my destiny."

Later, during the campaign, he made light of the fact that I had made this remark and repeatedly asserted that I had never disqualified him in any case prior to the time I became a candidate.

Dr. Gauthier, Rod Chambers, and I had a "council of war" and decided how we were going to approach the project. Since Rod, who had always been a booster of mine, was in the radio business, he of course favored heavy radio ads which Tom and I went along with.

In addition, we mapped out a newspaper campaign and Dr. Gauthier wrote the ads, always submitting them to me for approval prior to publication. I frequently made changes in the ads to stay within the constraints of the Fair Political Practices Commission. I had been advised by both retired Judge Joe Harvey and Presiding Judge Stephen Bradbury that a door to door campaign in Lassen County was a must if I was to upset the incumbent, Ridgely Lazard. Other cow county judges had told me the same thing.

In the Spring of 2006, the Children's Fair was held as usual and my secretary and good friend, Julie, who was quite familiar with the Children's Fair, orchestrated a booth at which the theme was (in addition to "Elect Don Sokol Superior Court Judge") fishing for the children with fake fishing poles. Behind a blind curtain various prizes were fastened on the lines with clothes pins by Julie. Debi and I stood there at the booth "barking" to the throngs of children and parents to go "fishing."

It was a huge success and probably garnered us quite a few votes.

Debra and I started our door to door campaign in the community of Westwood, Susanville's largest "suburb," by methodically going to every door in the community with campaign material, pamphlets, key rings, pens and other giveaways.

## Head to Head

The Candidates' Night programs in Herlong, Big Valley, Doyle and Westwood were in the form of debates. This gave me a forum to enunciate and explain my dissatisfaction with Judge Lazard's performance, particularly the *Turner* case.

In this proceeding Judge Gaylan Hathaway found him to be biased and prejudiced against three defense attorneys and unable to be impartial. I also raised the *Lemons* case which I felt Lazard's decision had resulted in a miscarriage of justice.

Judge Lazard accused me of being unethical for commenting on the *Lemons* case because it was "impending"—which it was not since the Judge had found there was no probable cause to hold Greg Lemons to answer on the charges and dismissed the case against him.

Since he dismissed the case, it was neither pending nor impending.

At the Westwood candidate's night, Judge Lazard bragged that, "I have never been reversed."

This gave me an opening that I had been waiting and prepared for. Years before when my son Taylor had been charged with possession of two bottles of Budweiser beer (a minor in possession) we had defended the case on the ground that the finding of the two bottles of Budweiser beer in Taylor's possession was the result of an illegal search and seizure. The bottles had been found in Taylor's pick-up one evening by a Susanville Policeman who had undertaken an interrogation of him in a parking lot because he claimed that he heard some suspicious noises emanating from the pick-up. He ordered Taylor out of his pickup after telling him that if he did not consent to the search he would be taken to jail and the pick-up would be searched in any event.

The discussion took the policeman five to ten minutes before Taylor finally consented to a search. It was our defense that Taylor was in custody at the time without being given his Miranda warning and without probable cause that any criminal activity had taken place or was taking place.

Judge Lazard found the search Constitutional.

We appealed to the Appellate Department of the Superior Court and three Judges from three neighboring counties ruled that it *was an illegal search and seizure and reversed Judge Lazard.*

I had these documents with me at the candidate's night in Westwood so when it came time for me to respond to Judge Lazard, I stated he was wrong about not having been reversed. I explained the case against Taylor and waved the decision in the air. In response to this, when it came time for Judge Lazard to speak, he arose and said, "There is no Appellate Department," and that what I had said was untrue.

This I found to be outrageous because my statement was true— he had been reversed.

After stating there was no Appellate Department of the Superior Court he added, "Anyway, it was just an opinion by three Superior Court Judges and not really an appeal"— or words to that effect. In stating there was no "Appellate Department" he was apparently hiding behind the technical distinction that *at the time* it was known as the "Appellate Division."

Thus went the nature of our campaign.

After the Westwood door to door campaign, we repeated the process in Doyle and Herlong. My sons Slade and Taylor came down from Boise and helped me expand the campaign door to door in Susanville.

On Election night I was very ambivalent about the outcome. We turned on the radio along about 7:00 PM. Debi and I were in the living room and Slade was in the kitchen with the radio listening for the returns.

He let out a whoop and a holler when the very first returns reported I was a few votes ahead, about ten.

That ten vote lead continued through the night.

Rod Chambers came by our house and we decided to go to the radio station where we listened to the returns first hand.

The count was not complete on Election night.

It was not until the next day, Wednesday, June 7, 2006, when the County Clerk phoned me about 4:00 p.m. with the news that I had won the election by one hundred eighty-three votes.

This was indeed cause for celebration.

**FDS with his Cessna 320 Skyknight,**
**Susanville California Airport, 2005**

**FDS swearing-in ceremony by Judge Stephen D. Bradbury**

**L-R FDS, Debra Sokol, Judge Bradbury**

**The Family of FDS in the jury box at his swearing-in ceremony.**
**L-R: Front: Eva, Christine, Mary**
**Back Row: Slade, Douglas, Robert and Taylor**

**New Judge Sokol in chambers.**
**Note Cowboy and Aviation Art in background**

# Chapter 31

## AFTER THE ELECTION
## MY ULTIMATE JOB

Although I had won the Election on June 6, 2006, under California law I would not take office until the following January 8th.

There ensued a period during which I was provided "bench guides" to study in preparation for my duties as Superior Court Judge. Also, it was necessary to finish all the cases that I could and to either sell my law practice along with the office if I could—or, as a last resort, sell the building without the practice and pass the unfinished cases on to other attorneys.

In the end, the latter is what had to be done because as soon as prospective buyers learned that the law practice for sale, which I had advertised in the daily legal newspaper (SanFrancisco Daily Journal), they became disinterested because of the "remoteness of Lassen County."

## *The Ceremony*

In preparation for the swearing in ceremony on January 8, 2007, I sent invitations to the entire family, that is, Eva, Douglas, Christine and Mary. Even Dorro said at first she would come to the event.

We also sent invitations to close supporters who attended in happy numbers.

It was a grand day with all six of my children plus my nephew Robert Converse in the jury box.

Many pictures were taken and we had a fine reception at our home.

## *Learning My New Job*

To become somewhat familiar with my new job, I'd followed another judge during the first week of January in all of the activities in Superior Court Department 2 where I would be presiding. But it was soon apparent to me that the only way to learn *judging* was to actually get in there and perform—mistakes and all.

The staff in Department 2 was wonderfully helpful and I got through my first calendar somehow.

In February 2007 I attended the New Judge Orientation Program (NJO) in San Francisco with eleven other new judges. It was a great learning experience and I gradually became more accustomed to the heavy court calendars.

In June of 2007 I attended the ten day Judicial College on the campus of the University of California, Clark Kerr Campus, with approximately 130 other new judges. It was a period of intense study and I made a lot of friends. We all have each other's addresses and phone numbers and it was made clear that we can call each other whenever needed for advice in puzzling situations.

Judging is the most challenging endeavor which I have ever undertaken. There is a real hazard as one makes difficult decisions as they arise, and to stay aware of any tendency to get the idea that perhaps one is smarter or better than most other people.

This, of course, is a completely erroneous position.

I must say, however, that as a group, Judges are good people in a unique position to help other people. Not only are we required to keep the populous from annihilating each other, but we can actually help other people in many ways. I had certainly not developed a settled style of judging after six months, but I kept working on it. Since no one thought I could win, the entire establishment of the Courthouse publicly endorsed Judge Lazard. Therefore, as I went about my daily duties, I was still uncertain as to my position with this "Courthouse Crowd"—of which I am now a member.

## *Fast Forward to 2013*

Here I continue my musing on the Saga of my life. It's Thursday, February 14, 2013.

So how did I get along with the "Courthouse crowd?"

As it turned out—beautifully.

The Courthouse employees and presiding judge, Stephen D. Bradley, were extremely helpful with only exceptions too minor to mention.

During the years 2007, 2008 and 2009 I was the Judge working in Department 2 with misdemeanors, preliminary hearings, infractions and on the civil side, civil limited (cases involving a $25,000 or less) and unlawful detainers. The Presiding Judge in Department 1 handled the big stuff like felonies, writs, unlimited civil cases and the Grand Jury.

During each of these years, I attended several Judicial training sessions and continuing education programs, most of which were in California but two weeks of which were in Chicago at Northwestern College of Law and two trips back to Ol' Miss in Oxford, Mississippi. These sessions in Chicago and Oxford were attended by judges from all parts of the country from the East Coast to the West Coast and it was a tremendous learning experience for me.

In the fall of 2009, I attended a course in San Francisco with respect to the Office of Presiding Judge. I did this because in California in two judge Courts such as Lassen County, the Office of Presiding Judge is supposed to alternate between the two judges every four years. Since I had only been a Judge for three years in the fall of 2009, I was just anticipating the job of Presiding Judge in another year.

## *Early Promotion*

Upon returning to Susanville from San Francisco, lo and behold, Presiding Judge Bradbury came to my chambers in Department 2 and as he entered the door, the first words out of his mouth were, "Well, you can have the job."

This was indeed startling news as he had told me earlier that he would remain as Presiding Judge until the completion of a new Courthouse which had been in the planning stages since 2002. In the fall of 2009, however, the construction had not been started and the Courthouse was still in the planning stage.

To say the least, it was gratifying to me that the Presiding Judge had enough confidence in me to turn the Presiding Judge job over to me one year short of my required four years. True to his word, he retired in January of 2010 and I took over the job of running the administration of the Courthouse with its forty employees and $4 million annual budget.

Judges assigned by the Chief Justice were brought in each week to handle my old duties in Department 2 and I took over Department 1 with its heavy duty calendar of felonies, unlimited civil cases and writs. I found that although the calendars were more congested in Department 2, that the Department 1 calendars required much more research and heavy duty decisions.

Since the Presiding Judge left office prior to the expiration of his term for which he was elected, it was necessary under California law that the Governor of California appoint a Judge to replace me. That appointee would be required to stand for election at the next General Election after his or her appointment. In this particular case, a new judge was not appointed until November 2010 at which time a local attorney, Michelle Verderosa, was appointed. She was sworn in December 2010 and took over Department 2.

## *A Heavy Decision*

I continued as Presiding Judge of the Lassen Superior Court in 2011 and 2012. Since my term would expire January 6, 2013, it was necessary for me under California law to run for re-election as an incumbent judge in 2012. The decision to run or not run had to be made under the law by February of 2012. I continued to debate in my own mind whether I should run for another six year term. I still had not made up my mind the day before deadline for the candidacy papers had to be signed before the Clerk of the County.

Two days before the final day to make the decision, Jon Nakanishi, the Family Law Facilitator and Court's research attorney, came to my chambers in the afternoon and told me he was thinking about running. He added that if I was going to run he would not out of respect for me.

The day before the decision had to be made whether to run or not, District Attorney Bob Burns also came and said he was thinking about running—but would not run if I was going to run, again, out of respect for me.

My respect for these two professionals was high and their comments most gratifying.

With these two leading contenders stating they would not run, I really had to rethink whether it was advisable for me to run for re-election.

In the final analysis, I decided that at my age of eighty-eight, it would not be advisable to run, and I should move on while I could "still smell the roses."

This decision was made on the basis that although I was able to do the job in a competent manner at the time in February of 2012, I could not honestly take the position that fate would allow me to finish the six year term of office, the completion of which would have me at age ninety-five!

Of course, the specter of having to shell out approximately $30,000 for a campaign with no assurance that I would win also factored into the equation of whether I should run for a second term. Further, I was devoting 100% of my time, almost, to doing the job including most Saturdays and Sundays for at least two or three hours each week in order to be prepared for the following week and its challenges.

I did not want to continue with this heavy work schedule until I dropped dead.

Should there be some break in life *to do as one pleases* prior to going to one's reward?

I've now had ten months of "semi-retirement" as I write these words, but I'm ready to *get going* again. The opportunity came when I was accepted into the California "assigned judge program."—more on this later.

**FDS presiding at the dedication of the new**
**Hall of Justice in Susanville, California.**
**At left, CEO of Lassen Superior Court Rosemari Reed**

**Daughters Evangeline and Mary with FDS "on the bench"**
**at new courtroom in Hall of Justice**

## Chapter 32

# NOT SINCE WORLD WAR II

W hile talking with my son Slade on the phone recently, the subject of this Memoir arose and during the course of the conversation Slade asked me whether I had included a chapter about our trip to Colorado Springs for a reunion of my old combat outfit, the Second Bomb Group of the 15th Air Force, 96th Squadron.

So here it is …

I had never attended former reunions of the Bomb Group who'd flown missions together in WWII so it was quite an event. We decided that Slade and I would fly the twin-engine Cessna 320 SkyKnight from Susanville and my other son Taylor would join us at Colorado Springs for the reunion. Taylor lived in Denver with his wife, Whitney, where they both worked in the wholesale food business.

Slade came to Susanville a few days prior to the trip. On August 17, 2011 we took off from Susanville about 6:45 AM bound for Colorado Springs. We climbed to nine thousand eight hundred feet for a smooth flight to Toole, Utah for refueling. It was about half way to Colorado Springs and to not stop for refueling was not a good idea.

As an old pilot (me) once said, "The only time I have had too much fuel was when I was on fire over Berlin."

We departed Toole with full tanks about 10:00 AM and climbed to eleven thousand eight hundred feet, having received a clearance from Salt Lake Center through Class C air space. We also got flight following information from Salt Lake Center for our flight over to Colorado Springs.

After passing Glenwood Springs, only about one hundred miles from Colorado Springs, I decided to climb to a higher altitude to have more clearance above the terrain lying ahead—some of the highest terrain in the Rocky Mountains.

As has been my routine, I moved the fuel mixtures forward and brought the prop RPM's up to climb power, twenty-five hundred RPM. About twenty seconds after this change in power, both engines started misfiring and were producing little or no thrust.

Five seconds more the left engine quit entirely and the right engine momentarily surged to full power!

During this brief period I switched the booster pumps first to high, which made the missing more pronounced, and then immediately back to low boost—but the misfiring continued.

I noticed the air speed rapidly decaying.

Suddenly the aircraft made an un-commanded pitch to the left.

It felt like we were going on our back and into a spin.

Since I had not entered commands for a spin, the airplane was actually telling me what it was going to do next.

My old Air Corp training came back (remember Nels Davis?) and I "dumped" the nose of the airplane abruptly in an attempt to regain control.

The air speed picked up and I was again in command of the attitude of the airplane—but with both engines continuing to misfire.

We had no more than three thousand feet to ground level although we were at about twelve thousand feet when the trouble started.

Slade had been following the flight closely on my *Foreflight* app for the iPad and I asked him to find the nearest airport.

He immediately said, "Aspen is at two o'clock to the right."

I estimated we were about ten miles from the Aspen airport and I turned toward it, telling Slade to contact Aspen Tower and declare an emergency—which he did, twice (just to make sure.)

The tower immediately cleared us to land, cleared the runway and held other traffic.

The engines continued to misfire all the was to touch down.

Reaching the runway seemed problematical all the way but the landing was "uneventful" and we were able to taxi to parking.

This entire episode consumed approximately five minutes from start to finish. I contacted the local fixed based operator and left the airplane with him to try to determine what the problem was. We all thought it was fuel contamination from the gas we put in the airplane at Toole, but this did not prove to be the case. To this day the cause of the misfiring has not been determined although at my nephew Robert Converse's suggestion, we had the magnetos pulled and sent to a magneto shop in the Seattle area. It was determined they were slightly out of time which may or may not have been the cause for the misfiring.

At any rate, Slade and I were able to rent a car and continue our journey to Colorado Springs where Taylor joined us as we spent several days reminiscing with a group of Second Bomb Group comrades-in-arms. Out of all the thousands that participated in the war effort with the Second Bomb Group, there were just twenty-two veterans present with only six pilots. The rest of the veterans attending were bombardiers, navigators and gunners.

These reflections are from notes that I made at the request of Slade on the very day it happened, August 17, 2011.

I taught both Taylor and Slade how to fly, and both have their private pilot's license.

Fortunate for me that day—and fortunate that Slade was my co-pilot!

# Chapter 33

# WHERE ARE THEY NOW

There is nothing greater than to see one's offspring grow to maturity, accomplish things, and be happy. I'm no exception, and I want to bring you up to date in 2013.

Evangeline Dorro Sokol, Aunt Eva's namesake, born May 15, 1949, graduated first as a physical therapist and then as a Medical Doctor. She is now a certified E R physician and has a small farm not far from Portland, Oregon. She has two children who travel extensively, as Eva does. We have frequent contact and she visits us for several days at a time, understanding that she is always welcome. I believe she also understands that I love her deeply as I do each and every one of my children.

Douglas Dooley Sokol was my oldest son, born March 7, 1951. You'll recall that he and I had the partnership in Sokol Vineyards, and that he stood by his dad, even when Dorro wanted him to join with my daughters and her in the trumped up lawsuit against me.

Douglas met with a tragic end on June 23, 2008, when he fell

**Eva's wedding on north lawn of Oxbow Ranch**

**L-R  Grandfather Dooley Converse, Eva, Jacko Garrett, Aunt Eva Battles, FDS.**

from a cliff above his mother's small ranch near Sisters, Oregon. He had been employed by his mother as manager of her ranch for several years after he had left the Napa Valley vineyards that he managed for the gentleman who purchased them from us.

During this period of employment he conceived the idea of developing about fifty acres of his mother's ranch into single and multiple housing units. The development was wildly successful and made millions for Dorro and my daughters, since Dorro had wisely placed the ranch into a corporation in which my daughters and Doug shared ownership.

It can never be accurately denied by anyone that Dorro has been generous and wisely managed her property to the benefit of our children—much more wisely than I have managed property and income which I have possessed.

Maybe, just maybe, fortune will smile upon me (Luck?) so I can yet do more in the way of property accumulation for the benefit of Debra and my remaining five children.

Christine, born June 16, 1952, is living in Sisters, Oregon, near her mother's ranch. Since she left the Broken Circle Ranch in Nevada—in which she was to have a partnership interest that was never consummated—has kept in touch but so far has never visited Debra and me.

I don't why.

She did come to my investiture as Superior Court Judge, for which I was grateful. Christine became a real cowgirl and "good hand" during her short tenure on the Nevada ranch. We had lots of fun roping those Mexican steers in the roping arena we built on the ranch.

Mary, born July 3, 1956, graduated in Law Enforcement from Southern Oregon University, and then earned credentials as a physical therapist like her mother and sister, Eva, had done. She has two children of her own and two step children from her first marriage. We communicate often and visit each other's homes. She is presently in Eugene, Oregon, where she lives with her physician husband. He's a great guy and contacts me frequently by e-mail as does Eva.

Slade Dean Sokol was born August 7, 1979 and grew up on the Broken Circle Ranch in Nevada, and in Astoria, Oregon and Susanville where Debra and I have our home. Slade graduated from Michigan State Law School in 2012 and is presently employed as an Attorney by a leading Boise law firm.

He graduated in the top ten percent of his class and the class book listed him as graduating "Summa Cum Laude"(with highest honors). When Slade got home to Boise after the graduation he phoned me and said, "Dad, I'm not entitled to the diploma "Summa Cum Laude" because I transferred from Cooley Law School—and transfers, even if they have the grades, are not entitled to "Summa Cum Laude" diplomas under the rules. I don't want that diploma hanging on my office wall because I would be misrepresenting myself to my clients."

I told him, "If this is bothering you so much, call the Dean and tell him your thoughts."

So Slade did just that and the Dean told him he was absolutely right and they'd made that same mistake with several other graduates, so return the Summa Cum Laude diploma and he would send him the correct one—a straight Doctor of Jurisprudence.

I believe the foregoing demonstrates what kind of a fellow our son Slade is.

When I told the story to a local attorney he said "He's too honest to be an attorney but he might make a good Judge."

I expect great things from Slade, and he will be assisted by his wife Kinsey who currently is a branch manager for JPMorgan Chase bank in Boise and on the "way up."

Taylor William Sokol was born September 28, 1982 in Elko Nevada and spent his first year on the Broken Circle Ranch, then Astoria, Oregon, and Susanville. He graduated from Boise State University with a degree in Journalism, but went to work for Con Agra, a food distribution company. He married his wife Whitney on July 31, 2010. Whitney was also employed by Con Agra Lamb Weston and they lived in Denver for a year or so but at the time of this writing have moved back to Boise where they purchased a house. Both are now employed by the J. R. Simplot Company, a global company engaged in the food production and distribution business. I am very proud of Taylor and his accomplishments. In my estimation, both he and Whitney are "on the way up."

## Chapter 34

# WINDING DOWN

I had the time coming in 2012 so I decided to go on vacation from mid-December of 2012 until the end of my term in January, 2013.

I must say it was with a heavy heart that I vacated my chambers in the new Courthouse which we had been occupying since the spring of 2012. I really liked the job but "time, which tricks us all" dictated that I leave office in an upright position— not feet first.

During the closing month of 2012, I filed the necessary application for sitting as an assigned Judge under the Assigned Judges program administered by the AOC (Administrative Office of the Courts) from San Francisco. This program furnishes judges as needed in various California Superior Courts to hear cases in which the local judges in each county are unable hear for various reasons, such as knowing the litigants or the attorneys too well.

I started this program January 7th, the day after my term officially ended, and thus far have handled cases in Butte, Siskiyou, Trinity, Shasta and Modoc Counties. I have cases pending in Modoc and Siskiyou courts and was appointed to one case in Lassen County in January 2013.

I must say this work has not kept me busy but I look forward to more "action" in the coming months and years.

As previously stated, I really miss being extremely busy.

At this point in time, Debra has an excellent job as manager of the Indian Health Clinic in Susanville and her income exceeds my retirement from the Superior Court and Social Security that I receive. Even so, our combined income is not as much as the approximate $180,000 I received as the Judge of the Lassen Superior Court.

Hey, I want to continue to have enough income to continue being able to financially afford my continued flying, but at this particular point in time I hesitate to fire up the bird because of the rising price of fuel. I have been trying for several months to sell my Cessna 320 Skyknight and obtain a single engine airplane. I'll even consider a trade for a single engine airplane.

In the meantime, life goes on and it remains to be seen how many more chapters in this *Saga* will be forthcoming. I really do trust that there will be several more and that they will continue to be in the exciting manner which have produced my story so far.

If not, it's still been a great ride!

CPSIA information can be obtained at www.ICGtesting.com
Printed in the USA
BVOW11s0615280514

354701BV00010B/75/P